T0147866

Get the FACTS

5 Secrets to a Healthy Christian Relationship from a Guy's-Eye View

Jermaine A. Hamwright

iUniverse, Inc.
Bloomington

Get the FACTS
5 Secrets to a Healthy Christian Relationship
from a Guy's-Eye View

iUniverse books may be ordered through booksellers or by contacting:

iUniverse
1663 Liberty Drive
Bloomington, IN 47403
www.iuniverse.com
1-800-Authors (1-800-288-4677)

ISBN: 978-1-4620-6628-5 (sc)
ISBN: 978-1-4620-6627-8 (hc)
ISBN: 978-1-4620-6626-1 (e)

Printed in the United States of America

Library of Congress Control Number: 2012901811

iUniverse rev. date: 2/14/12

For my little brother,
PFC Christopher M. Hamwright (1984–2009).
May you rest in peace.

Acknowledgments

First and foremost, I'd like to thank God, for calling me to write this book, and giving me the strength and courage to do so.

Thanks also to those military leaders who helped shape my character by instilling me with solid values: SFC Michael Christopher and SFC Dante Rayford.

Gratitude goes out to my schoolteacher, Miss Holmes, and Coach Collins (track coach), for serving as positive role models during my development.

Thanks also to my editors, Carla Fisher and Graciela Sholander, who both helped me grow immensely as a writer, in addition to dotting each *i* and crossing each *t*. This book would not have been possible without these two creative women.

Special thanks to my spiritual leaders — Chaplain (LTC) Milton S. Herring, Bishop David G. Evans, Reverend Ron Walker, Reverend James Betner, Pastor Barry Lyons, Pastor Dexter Coleman, Pastor Alain Tanoh and (my "Keep It 100" friends) Danielle, Amin, Danya, Andre and gospel singer Ernest Daniels Jr. — who offered me guidance and set me on my path.

Warm thanks to my family — my mother and father, Thelma Salder and Charles Hamwright; my sister, Chandra; my Aunt Pam and my Uncle George; and my Uncle Sam and my Aunt Barbara — for continuing to remain a big part of my support system.

And to all mothers and mother figures, I thank you immensely for your nurturing love, which has played a huge role in my life.

Contents

Chapter 3: Eliminate Guesswork with Communication

PREFACE
Essential Qualities for Lasting Love

*"The heart is a lamp with just oil enough to burn for an
hour, and if there be no oil to put in again, its light will go
out. God's grace is the oil that fills the lamp of love."*
—*Henry Ward Beecher*

Questioning the Question

I was talking with a couple of friends when the conversation turned to
relationships. A question came up:

"What qualities do you look for in a mate ... *besides love?*"

That caught me off guard. Not because I'd never thought about it
before. Like most men I know, I want a lifetime companion, a woman I'll
be happy to share my days with and proud to call my wife. I've put a lot
of thought into what I want from a relationship, and I've imagined my
dream woman often.

She's a woman of inner strength, confidence and grace. She'll put a
smile on my face and make me feel like I'm walking on air. As partners in
marriage, my special lady and I will support each other in our endeavors
and, if we're blessed with children, we'll work together to be there for our
kids. You can be sure that I've given the question of what to look for in a
mate serious consideration.

What caught me off guard was the last part of the question.

I almost blurted out, "What do you mean '*besides love*'?" Love is
what everybody wants in a serious relationship, and it's what keeps the
relationship going strong. If I don't love the person I'm dating, or she
doesn't love me, I'm not going to ask her to marry me. That would be
ridiculous. Love is definitely number one.

So if you have true love — a.k.a. the Real Deal — what more do you need? Does anything else even matter? Of course it does. The fact of the matter is that without five key elements, love won't last. I've seen way too many couples that started out loving each other break up over surprisingly mundane reasons. I've seen people who once loved each other with fierce intensity end up going separate ways because they didn't know how to get along on a day-to-day basis. Often, they're engaged in some sort of power struggle that dooms their union.

I know of relationships that fell apart because the loving couple failed to communicate clearly. Couples frequently break up because of misunderstandings, games people play, and feelings of being undervalued and unappreciated. Granted, there are many cases where it's for the best when two people go their separate ways. Either they're not compatible, or they're just not ready for commitment. I'm all for calling it quits versus being "stuck" in a relationship with little joy. But there are countless instances where the relationship *could* have thrived if only the couple knew the real secrets to success.

So even though love is a necessary, key ingredient for a relationship with staying power, love alone doesn't guarantee long-term success. There must be more. There must be a foundation for that love. That foundation is what inspired this book, and serves as its title. I'm talking about the FACTS. We'll get to them in a bit.

Let God In

Being a Christian has made all the difference to me, and I'm happy to base this book on values I've learned in Bible study that I've been applying to my relationships throughout my life. I know this book wouldn't even be possible had it not been for my faith. That's because of two reasons.

One, my ability to relate to people is God-given. Ever since I was a kid, I could sense things quicker than most people, and I'm also blessed with an incredible search engine-like memory. Even as a preschooler, I'd observe things like the daily flow of my parents' marriage and how they would respond to each other. While I didn't comprehend things at the time, as I got older, because of my gift of memory, I was able to process those events and figure out why things didn't work in their relationship (they divorced when I was in ninth grade). Having that memory gift is only half the equation; I am thrilled to be able to share it with you. While I don't have a medical background — and therefore don't have statistical case studies to present in these pages — what I do know is that this book provides you with a glimpse into the male mind. It's packed with advice I've learned from my own life experiences, from the trial-and-error examples of my friends and family and from the principles shared by my mentors. The lessons I teach form the tree trunk of any relationship, and they are foolproof. In fact, I once worked for a Christian radio station, answering caller questions on-air and teaching these concepts, and the satisfaction I get from helping others find what they're missing is immeasurable.

The second reason that faith is responsible for this book that you're reading is that, as a member of the U.S. Army for the past 10 years, even when my body and mind were tested by adversity, my faith is what kept me grounded, protected me and also gave me the time and solitude to come up with the FACTS. Seriously, military life makes you think a lot — when you're lying in bed at night in a foreign country, you really begin to discover what you're missing in life. And stateside, every time I'd get a new assignment and had to unpack in a new place, it felt as though the relationship-building clock was a-ticking. But I learned to appreciate what I have, so the Army actually bettered me in my relationships.

So I'm here to ask you today, when the road gets bumpy in your love life, who are you gonna call? Call on God! God will never, ever lead you astray. God loves you and your partner. He wants what's best for both of you, whether it's a satisfying, long-term relationship together, or a short-term friendship where the two of you learn valuable lessons and grow in the process. Maybe God wants both of you to go in separate directions so that each of you can find the person who's truly right for you. Trust in God who delights in guiding you and answering your questions. God knows best.

Unfortunately, there are many people who, in the heat of intimate desires, push God away. That's the last thing you want to do. Who created man and woman? Who knows our innermost desires better than we know ourselves? Who designed marriage? God did, of course. So trying to keep your hot and heavy feelings away from God is a big mistake. Invite God into your world always, even in the heat of the moment. Or maybe I should rephrase that: *Especially* in the heat of the moment.

God wants what's best for you and knows what's right for you. God can help you build upon the spark of love you have for the other person. Call on God when you need to stay honest, which includes not only telling the truth but also staying true to yourself. God can show you the weaknesses in your relationship and help you grow stronger in any of the

FACTS. Even when everything seems to be going great, don't hesitate to ask God for wisdom, clarity and discernment.

Like the Bible says in the quote that introduces this preface, put your faith in God and He will protect you.

The Basic Ingredients

All right, let's start at square one. What is universally expected in a satisfying, loving relationship? I maintain that there are two vital qualities everyone expects. These two ingredients are what people across the board, regardless of age, gender, or background, feel *must* exist in a good relationship. They are:

- **Love**: Genuine, heartfelt caring for one another. The feeling that yes, this is somebody I want to spend my time with and know intimately. Someone I would make sacrifices for, someone who'd make sacrifices for me. The person I enjoy being with completely, unquestionably. I am totally into this person, and the feeling is mutual.

- **Honesty**: The ability to share openly and talk with each other without feeling the need to hide anything. Being straightforward but fair, truthful but kind. Both people in the relationship feel they can tell the other person anything without being judged, condemned, criticized or ridiculed. Feeling like you and your partner can say what's on your minds. Feeling you don't have to pretend.

Without these two basic ingredients, a relationship doesn't stand a chance. You can look at a person and, from an intellectual standpoint, justify being with them; the person is attractive, nice, smart, has a good job, and seems to have it together. But despite all of these wonderful attributes, you're not going to be with this person for very long if love isn't part of the mix. You can be great friends, yes, but not boyfriend and girlfriend, and certainly not husband and wife.

Likewise with honesty. The person you're dating may be totally hot. You might enjoy yourself completely in this person's company. The two of you could have many interests in common. But if you can't be honest with each other, the relationship is doomed. Catching each other in lies, constantly making up (or hearing) excuses for being late or not showing up at all, avoiding conversations about stuff that matters, telling the other person what they want to hear instead of the truth — these are telltale signs of the kind of dishonesty that rips apart an otherwise good relationship.

Love and honesty, then, are must-haves, no question about it. Without them, a relationship won't last. These are the *basic* requirements.

But before you say, "Problem solved," listen to this: A successful, meaningful and long-term romance requires five additional attributes. These five attributes need to be well in place before true love and genuine honesty can even develop. What are these five attributes? What's still missing from the equation?

You Need the FACTS

Get the FACTS, my friends. That's the missing link. If you don't have the FACTS, you don't have a solid relationship. Real love and authentic honesty rely upon the FACTS as a foundation upon which to develop and grow.

These five attributes are just as essential as love and honesty. That's because if any one of them is missing, the relationship will struggle. Without them, your relationship will always feel as though it's lacking something. You may not be able to put your finger on it, but you'll know something isn't right. Ultimately, this dissatisfaction will grow and grow until both of you go your separate ways.

So if you want a relationship to stand a chance, you simply must have all the FACTS first. Only then can real love and honesty take root to carry your relationship to a higher level.

Beginning with Chapter 1, you'll get to know these components, one by one, and you'll be able to apply them to your own life, no matter your current situation.

How to Navigate This Book

The chapters of this book are meant to serve as a guide to being aware of the attributes that combine for a fulfilling love relationship.

Just as every human is different, every reader is different, and you might have two out of five attributes already and just need to explore those you're missing. Or you may have tried to include all five but didn't know how to put them into practice.

No matter which FACTS you already have or those you're lacking, you may choose to skip around to the most relevant chapters to you, while others would most benefit from reading it straight through. It's entirely up to you.

Just remember, we *all* have the capacity for the FACTS, and therefore, the capacity to find true love.

The Question Answered

Speaking of love, back to my friend's question: "What qualities do you look for in a mate ... *besides love?*"

Do you look for a pretty smile? Warmth and friendliness? Eyes that sparkle with the promise of adventure? A good sense of humor? Somebody with drive and ambition? A classy, intelligent person? A stylish dresser? A generous heart? No chip on his or her shoulder? A zest for life?

Those are all well and good, but you have to look beyond. Don't forget to look for the FACTS. Each one is so crucial to the success of a relationship, and in each respective chapter I've provided greater depth and ready-to-apply examples.

So, are you ready to take this journey toward deeply committed, lasting love? Great. Let's begin with the first FACT: **F**riendship.

CHAPTER 1
Friendship First

"Love is friendship that has caught fire. It is quiet understanding, mutual confidence, sharing and forgiving. It is loyalty through good and bad times. It settles for less than perfection and makes allowances for human weaknesses."
—Ann Landers

The Friendship Factor

Let's get something straight. I don't believe your partner has to be your best friend, at least not right from the start — it may take years before you regard your life partner as your best friend. But your significant other does have to be your *friend*.

There's no getting around it. If the friendship factor is missing, love and honesty are absent, too (and we've already learned how important those attributes are). You simply can't open up to someone you don't consider a true friend.

In the absence of friendship, your relationship becomes more of a business arrangement than an open, genuine bond between two people who care about each other and *want* to be together. What do friends do? They hang out together and have fun. They watch out for each other. They value their friendship and work to keep it going strong.

Real friends *like* each other. If you don't even like the person you're with, how can you ever hope to love them? So make sure your partner is also your friend.

The Job Search vs. the Search for a Soul Mate

I want you to reflect for a moment on your most recent job-hunting adventure. In particular, revisit the interview process. Who could forget the adrenalin-rushing, heart-pumping experience of being interviewed? No doubt you prepared well for your meeting, knowing that what you said and how you presented yourself made all the difference.

You didn't show up in flip-flops and a T-shirt, nor did you arrive without a clue about the employer. On the contrary, you dressed your absolute best to look the part, and you did your homework, learning all about the company and the position. When you spoke, you delivered the right amount of confidence — not too smug, and definitely not indecisive. You were selective about the information you shared, making sure to shine the best light possible on your accomplishments.

In your eagerness to get the job, you didn't reveal all. I'm not saying that you lied, but I'm sure you played up your strengths and decided to keep a few things hidden. We all do that, to a degree, in an attempt to keep the upper hand. While some people might never employ these eager-to-please job-hunting tactics, it's human nature to want to sound better than our résumé puts forth.

Let's say that a guy named Alan is in the middle of an interview. When the interviewer asks, "When can you start?" he replies without hesitating, "Tomorrow!"

Why did he say that? He hasn't even quit his current job yet. His answer is enthusiastic but entirely unrealistic. Since Alan believes this is what the employer wants to hear, he takes a chance and bends the truth, figuring the company won't bring anyone on board for at least another week anyway.

In another company's office, where interviews are also taking place, the hiring manager wants to know that Cheryl is familiar with a certain computer application. She answers, "Absolutely!" In reality, though, Cheryl's only heard of the application. She's never used it directly. Once again, in her eagerness to get the position, she stretches the truth and says whatever the employer wants to hear. She figures she can always learn how to use the application if and when it becomes necessary.

Neither of these candidates wants to admit any inadequacies — including, in Alan's case, lack of availability. Alan and Cheryl turned to stretching the truth out of good old-fashioned fear. Both are afraid that if the prospective employer finds out the truth, they'll lose their respective jobs to other more knowledgeable candidates.

That All-Important First Impression

The scenarios described above are not universal in the world of business, but they have certainly occurred, especially in more cutthroat industries. Like I said, it's human nature to want to convince the hiring party that we're right for the position. In our eagerness to get that job offer, we may cover up some things. We won't say, "I really don't plan to do any overtime." We won't reveal that getting up to speed will require a significant learning curve. We won't say, "I'm not a morning person, so don't expect much out of me until after 10 a.m." And we're certainly not going to point out that the interviewer is wearing non-matching socks.

Why? Because in a job interview, we want so badly to tell the interviewer what he or she wants to hear. Similarly, the interviewer might fail to ask the right questions and may only be interested in what we can do for the company. Either we get the job and learn quickly enough to stay on board, or we can't keep up and are soon replaced by someone else.

Take Matt and Jane, for instance. They've been dating for a while; however, both of them have been misrepresenting themselves to the other. They like each other a great deal, and both have already decided, "This is 'The One' for me." In an attempt to "get" the other person, each one is creating a false façade and hiding behind a mask, too afraid to reveal the true Matt or the true Jane.

Matt wants very badly to be the one Jane picks. He constantly tells her things about himself — some true, others exaggerated and others completely fabricated — to impress. Jane has already decided that he's the one for her. But she still puts him to the test, always asking in one form or another, "What do you have to offer?"

In time, this setup creates unnecessary tension between the two. Jane starts to suspect that not everything Matt says is true. This puts pressure on her to test him further, making him jump through more hoops. Matt starts to suspect that Jane doubts his ability to deliver what she needs, so he works harder to present himself in the image she wants. The demands increase, the deceit escalates and, in the end, the pressure's too much. The relationship stops being fun. Matt feels he can never meet her expectations. Jane feels she doesn't know the real him. Both tire of the games and go their separate ways. Had these two began their journey with honesty and friendship, instead of one-upmanship, they might still be together. First impressions are important, but not in lieu of relationship-building honesty.

Love Needs No Résumé

Many men and women treat their personal relationship like a job interview, but that's a big mistake. As we've explored in the examples above, each side picks and chooses what they reveal and what they keep hidden, often to ensure their professional life doesn't seep into their personal life. Each party wants to create an image and make that stellar first impression, and that may mean that each can't be perfectly honest about everything; it just wouldn't be professional to go on and on about personal problems. But in a love relationship, being on your guard all the time can spell disaster. If you try too hard to create an image, your partner will never know who you really are. If your partner hides behind a façade, he or she is not showing you his or her true self. Interpersonal relationships built upon false or ambiguous pretext is built upon shifting sand. Sooner or later, that castle you're building will crumble without warning.

Here's what I suggest: In your love relationships, don't demand a résumé, or pump up your own. Strive for an honest friendship. Get real with the person you're seeing. Get to the truth. And expect the truth out of them.

Too Much Professionalism Can Kill a Promising Relationship

For a number of reasons — anything from unrealistic expectations to insecurities to problems in past relationships — many of us, Matt and Jane included, are afraid to reveal the true self. Instead of saying what we really think or feel, we end up saying what our partner wants to hear. The relationship starts off on the wrong foot; it begins under false pretenses, and thus is doomed to fail unless both parties start getting honest with each other.

When emotional intimacy and authenticity is lacking in an otherwise promising relationship, things go wrong. There's a stiff formality present that prevents the two people from really getting to know each other in an honest way. An invisible wall divides them. They may not see this wall, but it's there. Down the road, this wall will create significant — maybe even irreparable — problems for the couple. The only solution is to tear that wall down before it's too late.

The Danger of Too Many Demands

For many people I know, the whole concept of dating and looking for a lifetime mate has been horribly distorted. There's a genuine fear of losing the "candidate," so the focus shifts away from getting-to-know-you sincerity and instead moves toward "sign here, please." A sense of desperation, perhaps, moves one or the other person to close the deal prematurely. Do these two people know they're right for each other? No, because they haven't taken the time and energy to become friends — real friends. Do they even know much about each other? Probably not, because they're too preoccupied with creating an image and/or making the other person jump through hoops.

For example, Ellen and Mark have been together about a year. Mark is about to propose to Ellen, and she suspects he will do so very soon. In fact, she expects he'll propose on Valentine's Day. She wants this. She wants it so badly that she's already telling him that the most romantic people in the world get engaged on this holiday. Ellen unabashedly tells Mark what type of roses he should buy her, and how many, and from which florist. She offers suggestions on how a man should propose to a woman. She even takes him to look at engagement rings, and she tells him her ring size. She makes it painfully obvious which ring she wants.

Now, Mark is a romantic at heart. He has his own ideas about how to propose. He was thinking about Valentine's Day, and he was thinking of getting roses. In addition, he's been making other plans. In fact, he's been pretty excited about the creative manner in which he plans to pop the question. But now Ellen is interfering with his plans. She's making all kinds of suggestions that weren't part of his original idea. As a result, Mark is growing discouraged. She's killing the joy of crafting his proposal and turning it into a business arrangement. Whereas he used to be excited about asking Ellen to marry him — in his own carefully thought-out way — Mark is no longer looking forward to it. He's not even sure he wants to marry her at all.

Perhaps Ellen doesn't trust Mark. She doesn't think he'll do the job right. She's afraid he's going to blow the important moment. Her friends' proposals were memorable, and she wants hers to be just as special. Mark, however, starts to resent her interference. He liked his ideas. He was comfortable with his plans. Now, he's worried that he won't live up to Ellen's expectations. He feels she's not supportive of him or his way of doing things. He wonders to himself, *Is this how it's going to be between us when we're married? Is she going to call the shots all the time? Will I ever have a say in anything?*

In the end, Mark doesn't propose to her on Valentine's Day. He postpones the proposal indefinitely. February 14 comes and goes, and Ellen is deeply disappointed. She wonders, *What happened? I thought it was a done deal.* What she fails to realize is that in trying to oversee the process and turn it into the most incredible, most perfect day of her life, she took away Mark's job. She kicked the creativity out of him. She took over the process and killed his plans. Their relationship now hobbles along, neither progressing nor improving. Both are stuck in a sort of limbo. The demands Ellen placed on Mark were just too much for him to deal with. She became the "boss" in a matter that she should have trusted her boyfriend to handle properly.

Does a Family Business Model Work?

The interviewer-interviewee business model isn't a replacement model and doesn't create a loving, committed relationship for many reasons, several of which I've touched upon already. But here's a question: Does the family business model work? I maintain that it works a little better. When you're interviewing with a close family member, say, to work in his or her business, your guard is going to be down. You don't need to impress. After all, this is somebody you've grown up with. This person knows you! Whether it's your mother or brother or aunt or cousin, you're close to this individual, and you won't hesitate to say what's on your mind.

If you can't start for another month because you're finishing up your current job, you'll say so. This gives the person a chance to work around your plans. If you want to work extra hours during the week in order to get every other Friday off, you'll be upfront about it and try to negotiate a deal with your relative. This person already knows a lot about you, including what jobs you've had, which ones you've enjoyed, which ones you've done well, and which strengths and weaknesses you have. You can be yourself during the interview. You don't need to hide, sugarcoat, protect or exaggerate. You can be very open and honest, saying, "This is what I'm willing to do, and this is what I'd rather not do."

So yes, a love relationship between a man and a woman shares some similarities with a family business model. In a personal relationship, as with a family business, you should be comfortable enough to speak with honesty, openness, dignity and respect. You should not have to sugarcoat or exaggerate things. There should be enough trust between the two of you such that you can say what's on your mind in a way that doesn't interfere with the other person's plans or step on his or her toes.

A professional relationship will *never* be exactly like a personal one. The two are different entities. Look for a friendship first, not a professional partnership. Grow in trust as friends before either of you starts calling the shots on how things should or shouldn't be. It's not like one of you is the boss and the other is the employee. You are friends looking to be partners in life, in love, even perhaps in raising a family someday. Neither one of you needs to micromanage the other. Business and friendship are not always compatible. When in doubt with your partner, pick friendship first.

Take the Pressure Off and Get to Know Each Other

So you're impressed with your girlfriend because she's got a fantastic job that comes with prestige and a healthy, steady paycheck. You're impressed with your boyfriend because he wears stylish clothes, drives an expensive car and has an MBA from Harvard. The two of you share a common vision for your future careers and your future together.

That's all well and good, but is she your friend? Is he your friend? How comfortable do you feel with this person? Again, bring this relationship back to earth. Take it down from on-a-pedestal status and bring it down to a real level. This, believe it or not, takes the pressure off. The best way to have a real relationship is to get to know each other — not behind images and facades — but for real. Think about it: Who do you feel more comfortable around, an interviewer or your buddy? Your HR manager or your best friend? Who can you get real with? With whom can you talk about what's on your mind, knowing that they'll accept you regardless of what you say? Your friend, of course. So naturally, you want the person you're dating to be your friend, not your supervisor.

Don't Love Like a Candle

A friendship is characterized by mutual feelings of trust and affection and the behavior that symbolizes a relationship between friends. In life, it's sometimes too easy to lose sight of this important fact. It's too easy to get caught up in the search for a mate who looks good on paper but may or may not be a good fit. In other words, we look for a résumé instead of developing a true friendship. We need to shift the focus back to the process of finding unbiased friendship. Only this can evolve into true love.

Sometimes it seems that we tend to love like a candle. We start out with a lot of fire. We get swept up by all of the feelings that come from our heart. The honeymoon phase is in full effect, things click and everything is great. But since we are burning like a candle, we burn hot and furious. And then, everything ends abruptly, just as a candle extinguishes the flame when it reaches its end.

It seems backwards that at the height of love we may feel less safe with the person we're with, but it is common for a few reasons. Relationships are fragile. Past hurts, rejection and fear can enter the relationship. It's cool to go down a road you've already been on, but when you get to the point of standing on new terrain, fear enters in. Without prayer, things get worse. Fear turns into needing more tangible things from that person, such as wanting to bring sex into the relationship. Or if sex is already part of the relationship, then the urge for it increases out of a need for strengthening a bond and an attempt to keep intimacy alive. However, the two people quickly find out that this extra element isn't the answer.

So what happens next? You start looking for someone else to help you. You start hanging out with friends, or you look for a new love interest. In other words, things spiral out of control and your current relationship dissolves. The amazing relationship you once had reaches an abrupt end. Suddenly, you completely forget what the honeymoon phase even felt like.

You also forget why you love that individual, or why you started going out with him or her in the first place. Small issues that were petty become major, and the relationship self-destructs. With that kind of love, I can see why it's so scary to love again or to even feel again. You start to wonder if maybe you've maxed out your ability to trust.

My advice to you is this: Don't love like a candle. Don't burn yourself out in the process. All this leads to is one big waxy mess that you're left to clean up! Take your time and get to know the person you're with. Do things together as friends. Again, take the pressure off. Don't start thinking about business-like arrangements, contracts and agreements. Don't jump into sex or commitment or areas that will complicate your growing friendship. Instead, think about doing things just for fun, for leisure. Come up with opportunities to chat and get to know each other. Enjoy simple things with each other — a walk in the park, an afternoon matinee, an hour at the coffee shop, a day at the zoo. Nothing scary or overwhelming, just normal stuff you'd do with a friend.

Always approach a relationship with optimism and hope. It never hurts to continually work on developing the friendship factor of FACTS. Your personal relationship doesn't belong in the competitive world of a job search. It's real life. Get to know your date or partner at a real, heart-to-heart level — one step at a time.

FACTS, Not Fiction: *Friendship*
You know you've got Friendship down when you feel comfortable sharing your thoughts and feelings with your special someone, without fear of judgment.

Do You Remember Why You Love This Person?

At the beginning of your relationship, something about your partner attracted you. Later on, as the relationship evolved, something about him or her made you fall in love. What was it? Could it have been his personality? Her strength of character? The way he supports you and your dreams? How she always has a compliment or kind word for you? The way he's passionate about a cause he believes in? The way she loses track of time when she's with you? His funny way of laughing? Her sweet smile?

Yes, there was something about this person that created a spark for you. But what was it?

The key to restoring your relationship when it's strayed off course and one or the other has lost the way is to remember why you love this person. Remember why you wanted to get to know this individual to begin with, why this person is special to you. What made him or her a friend, or at least, a potential friend?

When you approach your relationship as that of a friend, you can look at how your partner — with his or her or unique qualities — will add to your life plan, and vice versa. Do you have common values? What are they? Can you say to yourself, "This is why I love and care about you, because we're such good friends." When things get complicated or convoluted, go back to basics. Return to what you love most about this special person, this unique friend of yours, and the rest may start to fall into place again.

What Can I Do for You?

In a job interview, the underlying question always seems to be, "What can you do for me?" In your romantic relationship, you need to turn this question around. You should be asking, "What can I do for you?"

That's because part of the fun of being in a relationship revolves around what you can give the other person. And to feel comfortable as a giver, you need to let your guard down. This requires you to be confident in yourself, to like who you are.

Know that you're significant, regardless of what others think or say about you. If you think you're not valued as you truly are, you'll end up guarding your feelings. And when you're on guard, you can't give freely. You'll have closed yourself off.

Now, I realize we've all been hurt before, and this pain has a tendency to linger. Things might come up in a relationship that causes us to retreat within ourselves. In this state, we can't be givers. We're too busy protecting ourselves from getting hurt again.

Understanding this, I agree that yes, you must protect yourself. You can't just give blindly, thinking everything will work out fine. It's important to be realistic. If you're doing all the giving, and the other person is doing nothing but taking (and perhaps intentionally hurting you in the process), then you have to put an end to it. But don't allow past hurts to close your heart. Proceed with caution, but also with hope, with a willing heart, and with an open mind.

Take the past as a learning experience but, at same time, don't let how someone else treated before you rule your present relationship. This is a new relationship, a new start. Take a chance and rediscover the joy of giving with this person. Be confident that you're valuable and have much to offer. Trust yourself.

The Right Balance of Give and Take

Obviously, in any friendship there's a healthy give-and-take going on that adds meaning to the relationship. Striking the right balance is important. Give generously, and accept with gratitude. I can't think of a more fitting way to illustrate this give-and-take balance than through a couple of Bible verses. The first one is about giving generously:

> *"Remember this: Whoever sows sparingly will also reap sparingly, and whoever sows generously will also reap generously. Each man should give what he has decided in his heart to give, not reluctantly or under compulsion, for God loves a cheerful giver. And God is able to make all grace abound to you, so that in all things at all times, having all that you need, you will abound in every good work."*
>
> —2 Corinthians 9:6-8, New International Version

That's right, be a gracious giver. Don't give grudgingly. Give from your heart, and give voluntarily. Give cheerfully. That's what a friend does, and that's how you'll grow in friendship with your romantic partner.

Now, I'll present the other half — the taking part — modeled by the great teacher himself, Jesus Christ:

> *"Then he took the seven loaves and the fish, and when he had given thanks, he broke them and gave them to the disciples, and they in turn to the people."*

—Matthew 15:36, New International Version

From this Bible passage, it's evident that a good taker is one who is two things: gratitude and a willingness to share with others. So there you have it, straight from the Holy Book. In a friendship, the right balance of give and take requires giving with a cheerful heart, taking with gratitude, and being willing to share.

Friendship Cultivating Basics

We've covered a lot of ground in this chapter, but before we move on to the next element of the FACTS, I want to give you several practical ideas on how to go about being a good friend to your romantic partner. You do this by creating opportunities to foster your friendship. Here are several suggestions to get you started:

- **Focus on quality over quantity.** Come up with activities that will give you plenty of opportunity to talk. Go to the park — a public place where there won't be any pressure placed on either of you, where both of you can be yourselves. Find a park bench, or bring a picnic lunch and blanket, so that both of you can sit down and talk freely. Do simple but enjoyable things that allow for a high level of quality time, providing you with the opportunity to get to know the other person.

- **Consider volunteer work.** Volunteer in your community with someone you're interested in romantically, and you'll have an excellent opportunity to view that person's characters. Not long ago, I volunteered at a shelter preparing and packaging meals for the homeless. I brought along a lady friend to volunteer with me. We had ample time to talk, get to know each other, even understand one another on a deeper level. At the same time, we felt good helping other people. The joy we got out volunteering lasted all day long.

- **Explore a bookstore.** It may seem cheesy to some, but a bookstore can be a great place to take your date. With so many titles on the shelves, topics for conversation are endless! Bookstores usually have coffee shops and comfortable seating areas, the perfect setting for meaningful conversation.
- **Postpone the typical movie date.** I like movies just as much as the next guy, but I don't recommend taking a date to the movies at the beginning of a relationship, only because there's practically zero opportunity to chat. Instead, try going to a play. Typically, a play will have an intermission, giving you the chance to talk more during your date. Then, at the end of the play, you'll have an excellent conversation piece — yet another opportunity to get to know your partner better on a friendship level.
- **Be a tourist in your own city.** Other ideas for places to go with opportunities for conversation include: art shows, aquariums, zoos, institutes, museums. Also, any place where you can walk around and sightsee is great for inspiring light but honest conversation.
- **Get to know your love interest's family members.** Conversely, have him or her get to know yours. Interacting with your partner in his or her own element enables you to see your partner as he or she truly is, so make it a point to also hang out with your partner's friends, and he or she can spend time with yours. This way, you can see how he or she engages in a comfortable setting. Observe your partner in every light possible, and you'll have a better of idea of who he or she really is.

This list gives you ideas to get started. Feel free to expand the list and add more ideas of your won. Just remember to continue to try new things and keep finding ways to grow closer in friendship.

Keep It Light and Keep It Fun

Often, when you're seeing signs that your relationship is starting to dwindle, you need to realize that you're simply in new territory in this thing called love. Stop worrying and starting working towards making the friendship aspect of your relationship start to grow. All you really need to do is continue to see what God has in mind for you. By keeping things light and fun, you have a better chance of developing that important friendship.

Put all pretenses aside and start to get to know the person you're dating. Start doing things that friends do. Laugh together. Joke around. Have fun. Go out for a pizza or sushi or ice cream. Talk about what makes you happy, what scares you, what bugs you, what foods you like, what activities you enjoy, what books you read, what goals you have for your life. Find out what your partner is like and what he or she enjoys, what moves him or her, how he or she likes to spend free time, what his or her dreams are. In the process of getting to know each other, make sure to have fun. Keep things light. That's what friends do.

Keeping it light also keeps fear away. When you find yourself in brand new territory, it's only natural to feel different, uncertain of your next step, and even afraid at times. But get a handle on your fear. Don't let it take control of you. I've seen people do self-destructive things because it's easier to end the relationship than to face the unknown. It's like playing a video game; you're doing great, but then you reach a new, unfamiliar level and suddenly you don't know what to do anymore!

From what I've observed, it seems easier to break up and start over with someone new. A budding romance with someone else seems more appealing because moving to the next level of the current relationship will be complicated and takes skill. The next phase requires prayer, trust, faith and honest friendship, and these are skills few people have or comprehend.

Don't let it get to the point of sabotage and self-destruction. Focus on being friends and seeing where the relationship goes. Take the pressure off. Having a true friendship and being in love with someone who is your friend is a real blessing. When you're a true friend to someone, there's a greater level of understanding in that relationship. New territory is scary for many people, but the way to get beyond that fear is to be friends with the person you're seeing. When you're with a real friend, new territory isn't so frightening anymore.

True Friendship Keeps You Honest

Remember, your partner doesn't necessarily have to be your best friend — at least, not right from the start — but he or she should certainly be a *true* friend.

Keep your feelings true and your relationship fresh. Being a friend keeps the honesty in. It keeps both of you real so that you can treat each other the way the two of you want to be treated. Once you're genuine friends, you'll find it easier to master the next element of the FACTS: **A**ffirmation.

CHAPTER 2
Shine a Light with Affirmation

"There is no fear in love, but perfect love casteth out fear."
—1 John 4:18

Carry Your Love Like a Flashlight

This chapter is all about letting your light shine. Remember that song you sang way back in Sunday school? It went a little something like this: "This little light of mine / I'm gonna let it shine / Let it shine / Let it shine / Let it shine." That's what you're doing whenever you affirm your partner: You're shining your light so that he or she can see you fully. You're shining your light to help your partner find the way to your heart. This is an act of tremendous grace and kindness.

More and more, partners want to know if they're on the right track. Each person in a relationship has the power and responsibility to tell his or her partner whether he or she is on the right track or has veered off course.

Imagine for a moment you're inside a dark cave where you can't see a thing. Your partner is inside the cave with you, but you don't know where. You take a step, then another, trying to find your partner. Moving in the dark, you have no idea if you're walking in the right direction or if you're headed straight for a wall.

Here's the thing: Your partner has a flashlight. He or she can shine a light on your path so you can see clearly where you're going. But for whatever reason, the flashlight is off. You're walking blindly, and the other person refuses to help you. That's what it feels like when affirmation is missing from a relationship. You and your partner need to shine a flashlight for each other to help guide the way. You do this by affirming the other person, letting him or her know the way. On the other hand, you must also affirm sincere-but-misguided efforts, and then gently guide or nudge your partner back on track.

Through affirmation, both of you shine a light to show the way. When you walk blindly, without knowing where you're headed, that's exactly what it feels like when affirmation is absent from a relationship — and precisely why it is so necessary.

FACTS, Not Fiction: Affirmation
When your partner shines a light on your path to help you see the road you're both taking, and you do the same in return, you're practicing solid Affirmation.

The Path to Progress

Receiving affirmation is a way to check the box, so to speak — to gauge your progress and mark off milestones as you go. When you're being affirmed, when the light is shining so that you can see the path, you know you can keep going. Maybe you have to change course or take a step to the left or right, but at least you can see the path with clarity, allowing you to move in some direction without fear. You're growing.

But if you don't see any kind of light, and have no idea whether or not progress is being made, you'll get stuck. You'll feel frustrated, and you may not want to continue blindly through this relationship. Who would blame you? A relationship without affirmation isn't healthy. And everyone wants a little appreciation, recognition and guidance now and then.

Recharge with Appreciation

One important aspect of affirmation is appreciation. How hard is it to let the person you're with know you appreciate him or her? It isn't hard at all. And yet, so many people have trouble verbalizing what they value about their partner. This is where problems begin. If you're not appreciated, or at least you *feel* that you're not appreciated, what happens? Even a good relationship can become draining. Receiving appreciation is like recharging. All of us need to be recharged every once in a while. It's good for the spirit, good for morale and good for the relationship.

Maybe your partner is so good at being in the relationship that he or she makes it look so easy. Regardless, a thank you is still needed. He or she needs to know, for example, that you appreciate the little things. Look at the guy who likes to take his lady friend out to dinner, knowing just the right restaurant, ordering just the right wine to complement the meal. He seems to plan the evening effortlessly, but still, if his partner appreciates what he's doing for her, she should say so. This simple affirmation shows him he's on the right track, and the appreciation makes him feel good about himself. And when he's feeling self-confident, he's also feeling better about the relationship.

Or take, for instance, the young single mom who does wonders in the kitchen. Whatever she throws into the pot turns into a fabulous meal for her kids and her boyfriend. She prepares delicious fare with such ease and flair as though it's automatic. But again, just because she's good at it doesn't mean it involves no work. It takes plenty of skill, sacrifice, effort, careful thought and planning, along with the desire to serve something healthful and tasty to her loved ones. Her boyfriend needs to take a moment now and then to thank her for her wonderful cooking. Just because it seems effortless doesn't mean she doesn't deserve to be recognized. She's putting her heart and soul into these meals.

Whether it's a guy planning a romantic trip for his girlfriend or a woman getting perfect seats to the most anticipated basketball game of the season as a gift for her boyfriend — or any act of kindness shown by one member of a relationship toward the other — those gestures need recognition. Don't let the opportunity to thank your special someone pass you by.

Reach into Your Feelings

Perhaps one reason it's so hard to affirm your partner is it requires you reaching into your feelings. Telling somebody you appreciate him or her means you have to tap into your heart. Otherwise, the words will fall flat and carry no meaning. For many people, tapping into their feelings is a frightening, difficult task.

If you are such a person, my advice is this: Start at a place that's comfortable for you and build from there. If expressing appreciation and offering your partner reinforcement is difficult for you, don't try to do too much all at once. Start by saying thank you now and then. Thank your partner for a lovely evening. Compliment him or her on an outfit. Slowly but surely, start working your way up.

Begin to notice and appreciate nice things your partner says and does. As the saying goes, practice makes perfect. Once you start to get comfortable using affirmation as a form of expressing your feelings toward your special someone, you'll begin to view affirmation as a wonderful opportunity. Think of it as a chance to express your feelings and grow closer to your partner. It might be frightening at first, but in time it'll feel natural and it'll even feel good. Keep in mind that whatever you do for the benefit of your relationship can pay off for you and your partner in the long run. So get your courage up, tap into your feelings, open your heart a little at a time, and start practicing giving feedback and offering thanks. Keep actively practicing affirmation and appreciation, and not only will it become second nature to you, but also your partner will get valuable recognition from you.

Let Your Guard Down

Now, I realize that early on in a relationship, most of us are on guard. We are trying to impress, so we hold ourselves back. I advise you to overcome this tendency and let your guard down as quickly as possible.

You might ask, "How, exactly, do I go about overcoming this natural tendency to keep my guard up?" The answer lies in an element of the FACTS we've already discussed in great detail: friendship. This isn't just somebody you're dating. This person is your friend. Remember to keep this part in perspective. She's not your boss. He's not a stranger. Your partner isn't some mysterious, unfathomable entity you can't comprehend. Your partner is a real, live person who is also your friend. Treat your partner accordingly and you'll find it's much easier to let your guard down. When a genuine friendship is in place, the trust factor is present. And with trust, you can relax and overcome the crutch of putting up walls.

Another way to let your guard down is to balance your dates so that not all of them involve attending social events. It's fine to go out in public places with many people around and enjoy the social scene, whether it's a dance club, a church event, a family gathering or a volunteer event. But keep in mind that these events can be loud, distracting and demanding of your time. It's important that you balance these types of dates with quieter ones that allow you to talk and communicate, get to know your partner and earn a level of trust. Really getting to know the person you're with will help you to be yourself, instead of creating distance in the relationship.

I have to be honest with you and point out that all of this is easier said than done. Being open, affirming and trusting is something I have to work on regularly. I've found that when I am no longer in a relationship, I can be so honest with my feelings – saying what I appreciated about her, even pointing out what I liked and didn't like. It's as if the pressure is suddenly off; it's over now, so I don't need the façade anymore. And I end up becoming best of friends with this lovely individual because we've moved past the idea of being hurt.

Yes, your ex can become your good friend. But I invariably shake my head and lament, "If only it was this way when we were together!" The truth is that it can be this way, but it takes diligent work. It is definitely worth the effort.

Allow a Learning Curve

It's been my experience that women appreciate it when a man takes the lead. They like it when he plans a nice romantic date and takes care of all the details, from picking the right restaurant to bringing a bouquet of flowers. And for our part, we like to surprise our date and give her special treatment.

Problems arise, though, when a man isn't allowed a learning curve. If he's expected to do everything perfectly from the start, even before he has a chance to discover what his date likes and dislikes, he will soon feel defeated and dejected.

Here is where affirmation and communication are once again important. For any women reading this, it's important to know that if your man is doing a great job, you should affirm his behavior by telling him so. And if he's not doing so well, but you know he's trying, then affirm him by letting him follow a learning curve. I don't recommend expecting him to get every detail right the first or second time around. Like schoolteachers do with their pupils, reward good effort, then gently guide him without discouraging him. There should be granted the leeway to make a mistake or two so he can learn and do better next time.

When I was in the Army and I first became a non-commissioned officer, I knew nothing about leadership. At the time, I misused the power and responsibility I'd been given. I tried my best, but failed many times. The good news is I've learned a great deal from all of those failures. In the long run, I was glad to have been given that learning curve. In the end, I became an effective leader.

It's the same with any relationship. A leader emerges when he's given the chance to learn from his mistakes. Sometimes, men aren't given the opportunity to practice. They're expected to know everything from the start and do things perfectly. One slip-up on his part and that's it, the woman feels she must take control. In turn, the man feels she doesn't trust or support him. This isn't a good learning environment. He eventually lets her take over, which creates an imbalance of power and makes a man feel emasculated. This leads to tremendous frustration on both sides. He feels he can never do anything right, and he's hesitant to even try. She feels he can't do anything right, and she takes control but secretly wishes he would take charge. As you can imagine, this scenario can spiral out of control to the point in which he begins to resent her and she feels she's got a child — not a man — in her life.

So, ladies, keep this important fact in mind: Men can't be perfect from the start. Guide your man when necessary, offering your gentle support, but let him make a few mistakes so he can learn from them and improve. And trust that he will, in time, learn. You'll be glad you did.

Making Gentle Corrections

Affirming doesn't always have to be telling your partner that he or she is doing something good. Affirming can be about gently nudging him or her in the right direction when expectations aren't met.

This can be as simple as stating your likes and dislikes. In the previous chapter, I discussed how some people may approach a personal relationship as though it were a job interview. I pointed out how this tactic doesn't work. When you offer affirmation, be sure not to hold back, as you might with your employer or someone who's interviewing you. Instead, be honest — in a kind way, of course. It's all right to redirect your partner through gentle, loving honesty:

- **Gentle Correction 1:** "Oh, honey, that is so sweet of you to buy me chocolates! You are very romantic. I appreciate your thoughtfulness immensely. But if we're going to be in a relationship, you need to know that I dislike chocolate. Now, don't feel badly; I never told you this before, so you had no way of knowing! But chocolate just doesn't agree with me. So I'll accept your generous gift, but please do not buy me chocolates in the future."
- **Gentle Correction 2:** "What a wonderful surprise this trip is! I had no idea you were planning something so special for me. How long has this been in the works? You really put a lot of time, thought and energy into this trip. Thank you very much; I greatly appreciate what you did for me. I need to let you know, however, that I really don't like snow. I am freezing my tail off here. Please don't take it personally. I'm just letting

you know that as much as I am deeply touched that you care enough about me to arrange this lovely trip, I would much rather have a picnic in the park or take a stroll along the beach than drive up to the mountains to see snow."

- **Gentle Correction 3:** "You know I truly admire your intellect. You know so much about so many different subjects. My only request is this: Please take a moment to listen to some of the points I'm making. I know you get very excited when we're talking about a subject you know so much about, and I appreciate the passion you exhibit, but I'd like to be a part of the conversation as well, so please allow me the opportunity to state my point of view."

Do you see how in each example the speaker doesn't hold back his or her feelings? With kindness and compassion, true sentiments are expressed. This type of affirmation can be classified as *gentle corrections*. In each case, something is appreciated — the person's effort, generosity, intellect, the gift that was given, the gesture that was made. But also in each case, gentle corrections enable the partner to learn more about likes and dislikes. It's critically important to communicate your true feelings in a relationship, but it's just as important to communicate these feelings and sentiments in the kindest, most positive light possible.

Be Direct and Don't Sugarcoat

If there's something you don't particularly like about your partner's behavior, don't be afraid to speak up. Holding information back makes thing worse, escalating to the point where it puts your relationship at risk.

Always stay respectful and dignified. Remember, it's OK for either of you to say, "I don't like chocolate; I like flowers," or even, "I don't like red flowers; I like blue ones." Both of you have every right to say, "I appreciate your thoughtfulness in taking me to the movies, but this type of film isn't really for me." There's no need to sugarcoat. Be direct. Achieve a deeper level of honesty and your relationship will be stronger in the long run. Simply treat others the way you'd like to be treated.

Aim for a Level of Constancy

Have you ever spoken up about something to your partner and then worried that he or she will yell at you? But instead, they listen and simply respond, "OK." Wow, doesn't it feel good to make this type of breakthrough? Suddenly the frustration you've been feeling is gone. The anger and resentment that had been building up begins to fade away. You're so grateful that somehow you summoned the courage to speak up!

Try to not let things get to the boiling point. Don't get so frustrated that you're about to have a breakdown. Instead, affirm regularly, little by little. The key to affirmation is constancy. You want to give your partner feedback on a regular basis. If you wait until the relationship has built up so much tension and is about to self-destruct, then you've waited way too long to offer affirmation.

Don't worry, you won't be mothering your guy by expressing gratitude for the stuff he buys you or by assertively saying, "This is a sweet gesture, but you're a little bit off track." And guys, don't worry — you won't be a fool in your gal's eyes if you tell her how much you appreciate the sweet things she does for you, like baking you cookies or being especially nice to your parents.

Affirmation is a good thing. Do what you feel in your heart rather than trying to impress the other person or trying to look cool. It's easier to affirm honestly and kindly when it comes from the heart, instead of doing it just for show.

Affirm Early and Often

When you don't know where you stand, chances are you'll want some sort of proof or feedback. It's like being in school and doing the work, turning in all your assignments, but the teacher never grades or returns them, so you have no idea what your current grade is. As a result, you end up doing more work, submitting all the extra credit you can, because you're uncertain of where you stand. When you finally learn you're getting an A in the class, you relax. "Phew, I'm doing better than I thought," you think, "so I don't have to do the extra credit anymore. I can coast for a while."

Well, folks, it's like that with relationships, too. When a guy doesn't know where he stands with a girl, it can drive him crazy. He wants to know where he's at in the relationship, so he'll work extra hard — bringing her flowers, taking her out to special places, getting her little gifts. He's doing all he can to win her over, because he's scared he's not making the grade. Once he finds out he's doing fine in her eyes, he relaxes … and she grows disappointed, because suddenly he's not as attentive anymore.

I've heard many women ask variations of the question, "This guy started out this way, but now he's that way. What happened?" I hear the deep disappointment and confusion in women's voices when they state, "After I told him I care, he backed off. Why?" Or even, "After we had sex, he changed. Why is that?" It's frustrating and heartbreaking to hear these genuine grievances. But the answer can be provided with one word: affirmation.

When a man doesn't feel validated or affirmed, he may try to conquer, and he'll do this in one of two ways: Either try to buy his girl's love through expensive gifts and outings, or try to pressure the girl to sleep with him. I'm not saying this is right; I'm just pointing out that this is how it is. It's a form of insecurity. Then, when he finally determines that he's doing well — that he's getting an A, so to speak — he holds back. He feels he doesn't have to work so hard anymore. He stops giving her all that attention, the flowers, the gifts. He places fewer phone calls, texts her less and less. Even intimacy declines, because he figures the two of them are "cool." Now the girl is going crazy wondering, "What happened? Why did he change? What did I do?"

To avoid this situation, here's my advice: Give affirmation early, and give affirmation often. This way, the pressure will be off and disappointments will be avoided. Affirmation serves as a much better barometer than the man's attempts to win her over. This leads to a more comfortable, realistic relationship, without uncharacteristic behavior on his part, and with less pressure and fewer disappointments for her.

This Little Light of Mine

After friendship, I believe that affirmation is the most essential, most necessary element of FACTS. Remembering that song from earlier in this chapter, I'm also reminded of the Bible verse in which Jesus is giving his Sermon on the Mount and speaking of letting one's light shine:

"You are the light of the world. A city on a hill cannot be hidden. Neither do people light a lamp and put it under a bowl. Instead they put it on its stand, and it gives light to everyone in the house. In the same way, let your light shine before men, that they may see your good deeds and praise your Father in heaven."

—Matthew 5:14-16, New International Version

That's right, let your light shine before others. Let your light shine so that others may see who you truly are. Let your light shine in front of your partner so that she or he can see your true self, and so that your light may help guide the way in your relationship.

Affirmation in Action

To recap, here are some ways you can effectively affirm your partner:

- Show appreciation for the wonderful things your partner does for you, even if they don't seem time-consuming or aren't quite what you expected or hoped for.
- Thank your partner, often and sincerely.
- Tap into your feelings to share honestly from the heart.
- Offer your partner some pointers and reinforcement, as well as feedback, on a consistent basis.
- Express your feelings to your partner so the two of you can grow closer.
- Treat your partner as a friend.
- Gently correct your partner when necessary, nudging him or her in the right direction, explaining what you like and dislike.
- Shine a light for your partner so that he or she can better navigate through the relationship and you can both move forward and grow.

If you don't act as you truly are, you won't be happy. And you want to be with someone who wants you as you truly are. At the same time, it's better for you when your partner speaks her or his mind. It will give you the chance to know where you stand, and this in turn will put you at ease.

The Joy of Reciprocity

A relationship really is like a cave, especially in the beginning. Both of you are maneuvering in the dark, trying to find one another, trying to reach the other person.

Affirmation is the light inside this cave, the beacon you shine for each other so that you know where to take that next step. The more you understand the person you're with, and the more that person shines a light on your path, the more you'll feel comfortable with him or her taking the lead. The opposite is also true: The more the other person understands you, and the more you shine a light to help that person see the way, the more comfortable he or she will feel with you. This opens the door to greater trust, better communication and even more support for each other. Shining a light for each other is about keeping each other's best interest in mind often, if not always.

The Next Step

Now that we've covered how to develop a genuine friendship with your romantic partner, and how to affirm each other in a relationship — the F and the A of FACTS — let's move on to the next important element: Communication.

The art of communicating is a skill you'll want to develop early in life. It will serve you well in every area of your life, but especially in your love life.

CHAPTER 3

Eliminate Guesswork
with Communication

*"You can't stay in your corner of the forest waiting for others
to come to you. You have to go to them sometimes."*
—A. A. Milne

In the Beginning ...

Anthony and Alice were crazy about each other the moment they first
met at a party. They exchanged phone numbers and soon started dating.
They discovered they have many common interests, from a passion for
volunteering in their community to a fondness for gourmet pizza. For this
pair, it was love at first sight.

Five months later, the relationship is hanging by a thread. It's Saturday
night, but instead of spending time together, each person is doing his or
her own thing. Alice is at a coffee shop with a couple of girlfriends while
Anthony is home playing video games with his buddies. Neither one knows
when they'll get together again. Despite that initial passion, things have
cooled off. What happened?

Assuming, Not Communicating

Yes, Anthony and Alice were remarkably compatible. Neither had
ever met someone this compatible before. Sensing that this had to be It,
they jumped into a relationship without first taking time to get to know
each other. Soon Alice was making plans for the two of them, figuring
their future marriage was already a done deal. She talked nonstop about
where they should live, how many hours each should work each week, how

much money they should make as a couple, where they should go for their vacations, how many children they should have, who should stay home with the children, and on and on. Anthony listened but said nothing. He grew increasingly uncomfortable. Alice didn't seem to notice his growing uneasiness.

Instead, she kept talking, and Anthony kept listening quietly, but neither was communicating. Without him ever mentioning marriage to her, she assumed it was a given. It's true that he had thought about marrying her, but the more she talked about it, the further away she pushed him. He resented her for making these assumptions about spending the rest of their lives together without first consulting him. Didn't he have a say in the matter? The more she planned out their lives, the less interested he became.

Soon, Anthony was back to hanging out with his friends, leaving Alice to complain to her friends about what a loser he turned out to be. What broke this relationship up was a lack of genuine communication, the C component of FACTS. Love at first sight can't sustain itself for the long haul when poor communication exists between the couple.

FACTS, Not Fiction: Communication
In order to Communicate effectively, both partners must be good speakers and sensitive listeners.

The Mind-Reading Myth

Anthony and Alice got off to a promising start. They went in with good intentions and high hopes. But the reason the relationship came to a disappointing end was that something essential was missing. They failed to *communicate*. She assumed too much without checking with him, and he remained silent too often, giving her the impression that they were connecting.

Both verbal and nonverbal communication must be ongoing in a satisfying, whole relationship. It's important for each person to state matters clearly without trying to make the other person guess what one is feeling or thinking. The statement "If you loved me, you'd know what I'm thinking right now" couldn't be more of a myth. Unless a person is a highly skilled mind reader, there's no way he or she can know what the other is thinking.

That's why it's crucial for both partners to communicate regularly. That's why each person must tell the other person what's going on.

Until we humans develop the capacity to fully communicate with each other on a nonverbal, completely intuitive level, we need to become good talkers *and* good listeners. Effective communication is a two-way street. The listening part, which many people need to improve upon, is as important as the talking part. In this chapter, I'll offer pointers so you can advance your skills in both.

Where Do You Stand?

When you're trying to live a godly life, you need to know where you stand. What do you believe? Which values do you embrace? What can you live with? What won't you tolerate? It's important to let your partner know where you stand, both in your life and in your relationship. Don't play games with her. Don't hide the truth from him. If you both want a solid relationship blessed by God, then you must be forthright and upfront about what matters to you.

If you don't know where you stand — and on top of that, you have no idea where your partner stands on issues and principles that matter to you — then the two of you will only run into trouble. Knowing where each of you stand on important matters involves effective communication, honesty, trust and support. Also key elements are love, friendship and affirmation.

You should feel comfortable saying to your partner, "Hey, here's what I think about this. I feel pretty strongly about it. How about you? What do you think about it?" By being honest in your communication, you feel comfortable to say what you really believe, not what you think the other person wants to hear. But you do so respectfully, because you love this person. By putting the love you feel out there in the forefront instead of hiding behind masks of defenses and fears, you'll know exactly where you stand in the relationship.

Recognizing Poor Communication

More problems arise in a relationship because of poor communication than incompatibility. People would be more compatible if they learned how to talk and listen to each other in real, meaningful ways. Your goal, of course, is to acquire the skills needed to foster good communication between you and your significant other, whether that person is a brand new love interest or a life partner you've known for years. In addition, learn to recognize poor communication so that you can steer clear from it.

Take, for instance, Danielle and Justin. The pair has been dating for several weeks. Both are nice, intelligent people with much going for them. They find each other attractive, and they share several interests. Lately though, they've been running into dead ends in their relationship. Trying to be polite, and not wanting to rock the boat, neither has been saying what's really on his or her mind. As a result, they're unintentionally keeping each other in the dark. Because neither one speaks up, resentment builds, confusion reigns and incorrect assumptions are made.

One night, Justin calls Danielle and asks her out to dinner. He says he'll come over at six. She says that'll be fine. He arrives, but she's not ready to go. He waits 10 minutes, 20 minutes, 30 ... all the while looking at his watch and growing increasingly frustrated. Finally she appears, looking radiant. Justin wants to say something about how long she kept him waiting, but he lets it go.

The couple heads out to a place where they usually dine. Danielle isn't thrilled, since she was hoping they might try a new place, but she keeps this to herself. He orders an expensive bottle of wine for the two of them. She barely takes a sip, smiles politely and orders iced tea. The expensive wine sits there in her glass all night, untouched. Nobody mentions it, but Justin secretly feels Danielle is too finicky. Doesn't she appreciate fine wine?

They order their meals and eat mostly in silence, both of them visibly bothered by something. Neither one says what's on their mind. Neither asks the other what's wrong. After a rather dull, uneventful evening, Justin takes Danielle home. They kiss goodnight, and he drives home to watch television by himself. The two have a few more dates, but the spark seems to be gone. Their dates have become boring and tedious. Without saying much, the two decide to part ways.

What happened to this relationship? Basically, a lack of communication killed it. Both Danielle and Justin had unspoken expectations, and both ended up with resentment buildup. Justin felt it was rude of Danielle to keep him waiting so long while she took her sweet time getting ready for dinner. He resented having to sit around doing nothing but wait for 30 or 40 minutes. It gave him the impression that Danielle did not value him or his time, and this made him angry. However, he kept all of this to himself.

Danielle didn't realize she was being rude. She felt it was polite to let Justin come over whenever he wanted. If he said he was coming by at six, that was fine by her. She assumed that he knew she got off work at 5:30, arrived home just minutes before six, and needed a good half hour or longer to get ready for dinner. Danielle made her assumption without ever specifically communicating any of this vital information with him.

Justin wanted to be a man in charge, so he always chose the restaurant and tried to impress his lady with expensive wine. Danielle is a vegetarian and isn't a wine drinker, but she didn't want to seem like a complainer, so she never suggested another restaurant and never declined the wine he bought. Justin certainly noticed that she didn't seem happy during their dinners together, but he never asked about it, and she never offered an explanation.

Both secretly came up with conclusions about each other that inevitably brought about their relationship's demise. Justin concluded that she was a selfish prima donna whom nobody could please. Danielle decided that he was an arrogant, self-centered rich guy who liked to wine and dine his lady but didn't care about getting to know her.

What's Really Going On?

Were they right about each other? No, not even close. The truth of the matter is that they're both decent, reasonable people, but their serious lack of meaningful communication has led to grim misunderstandings. Danielle isn't a prima donna; she genuinely needs time to get ready before a date, and five minutes just isn't long enough. But afraid of offending Justin, she failed to speak up and explain the situation to him.

Being a vegetarian, something Justin never noticed and she never brought up, Danielle has a difficult time finding meatless options in certain restaurants. The place Justin typically chose for their dates offered almost nothing in the way of vegetarian fare, making dinners with him a source of disappointment and frustration for her. In addition, Danielle never had a taste for wine. She'll have a cocktail, but doesn't care for wine. Realizing that Justin was trying to impress her with an expensive bottle, she politely took a sip but could not bring herself to drink more. She never said a thing about her needs and preferences because she wanted to go with the flow. The resentment, however, gradually built up inside her.

It's clear that Justin wants to be the kind of guy who takes good care of his lady. He doesn't want to appear wishy-washy in any way. So instead of asking what time he should pick Danielle up, he made it his habit to tell her what time he was coming over. Instead of asking for suggestions on where to go for dinner, he made the decision himself, usually picking the same place simply because he felt most comfortable there. Justin isn't arrogant, self-centered or wealthy; he's a painfully shy person working hard to make ends meet. Both his shyness and his desire to "take care of everything" prevented him from asking Danielle anything about her preferences. In the end, Justin felt she rejected his attempts to impress her. He never discovered that there was a logical, reasonable explanation for her unhappiness during their dates. A healthy dose of communication would have changed everything for these two.

How to Avoid the Guessing Game

A relationship becomes very difficult to continue when both parties are forced to play a guessing game. Resentment builds, frustration grows and assumptions are made that are far from the truth or reality of the situation. Forcing one's partner to guess is unfair and impractical. Each person must speak openly and plainly. At the same time, both partners must take the time to listen to the other person — I mean *really* listen — giving each other full, undivided attention.

Both people must be willing to listen to the words as well as the *feelings* behind the words. For example, notice when your partner has tears in her eyes or fear in his voice. Never be afraid to sensitively ask, "What's wrong?" simply because you don't want to rock the boat or because you're afraid of it resulting in an argument.

How much easier it would be if we learned to talk and ask each other important questions! If we could move away from the guessing game and move into a "let's talk" mode, we'd know each other so well. We'd have a better idea of where the other person is coming from. This would open doors to a deeper friendship, increased trust and understanding, and both sides showing greater support for each other.

In a relationship you can't help but guessing and jumping to conclusions when effective communication is absent. When you hear your partner say or imply something, your mind strives to make sense of the information, telling you, "I think that *this* is what they meant." But you don't have the whole picture, so your conclusion isn't always accurate. This is especially true when you start getting upset and allow your mind to go wandering down destructive paths. Reason goes out the door as you begin thinking, "Maybe they did this on purpose. Maybe they did this to hurt me." Stop yourself right away! This is known as head trash, and more likely than not, you'll find that your fears are completely unfounded.

This is one of the reasons that communicating is so important. You don't always know what the other person means. You don't always know why your partner is behaving a certain way. This is why you need to speak up and calmly ask for clarification. Otherwise you become judge and jury without finding out what's really going on. Take the guesswork out of your relationship. There's a very simple, straightforward method of doing this. It's called talking and listening.

Communication is two-way street. It's a give and take: You talk a little, and then you listen. Your partner says something, and then she or he listens. Do you ever have phone conversations with someone, maybe a friend or a relative, where you can hardly get a word in edgewise? The other person talks and talks and talks some more, dumping everything that's on her mind, and before you can respond she finishes with "talk to you later." You feel cheated out of a satisfying conversation, right? Effective communication can't be this way; it has to be a two-way deal. Good communication isn't about delivering information — it's about sharing, which involves both talking and listening.

The Dangers of "Always" and "Never"

I once heard a pastor say that there are two words that should not be used in an argument: never and always. When you think about it, this makes a lot of sense. Statements such as the following are untrue, dishonest and can make the other person feel defeated and withdrawn:

- "You *never* get this right."
- "You're *always* messing up."
- "You *never* listen to me."
- "You're *always* late."
- "You *never* think about the consequences."
- "You *always* embarrass me."
- "You *never* care about what I think."
- "You *always* forget to call me."

Nobody likes hearing statements like these. *Always* and *never* statements immediately put the recipient on the defensive. What's more, nothing gets resolved through such accusations. These statements are unreasonable, unkind exaggerations. In all of your dialogues with people, stay away from such statements — and take special care that they don't enter your love life.

Whenever you feel like you're about to blow up and shout out an *always* or *never* accusation, stop yourself, take a deep breath or two to calm down and let the other person know that you need some time alone. Go for a walk, or just leave the room for a few minutes. Take the time to regain your composure.

Using "I" Statements

In a reasonable manner, think about what is bothering you. What's making you mad? Why are you upset? Then, in your mind, phrase your thoughts and feelings in such a way that you're not merely accusing or attacking the other person. Here are examples of how you might phrase the reason that you're upset. Remember to use "I" statements so you do not blame:

- "I'm upset because I thought I made it clear that I'm very allergic to dairy products, and you're taking me out for ice cream."
- "I'm disappointed because we agreed to meet at five, but you didn't show up until seven."
- "I'm sad because I feel you're not hearing what I'm saying."
- "I'm mad because I had to wait 45 minutes for you today, and 30 minutes last week. I like promptness. I don't like to keep waiting."
- "I'm unhappy because my opinions don't seem to matter."

These statements communicate exactly what you're feeling and why, without attacking the other person. They express your disappointment, anger or sadness, and they address a specific instance or issue. Now you've got something tangible to work with. Now you're communicating. The other person has genuinely valuable information to process. What he or she does with this information is up to her, but at least you have calmly expressed how you feel and why you're hurt, and you've done so in a reasonable manner without attacking your partner. It's a good start to problem resolution.

Don't Hold It In

There are people who internalize their thoughts, feelings and emotions. They say nothing, even though something is really bothering them. Instead, they store everything inside, and they keep adding to it over time. Imagine having a partner like this (maybe you don't have to imagine too hard). Every time you do something that bugs him, he keeps quiet but adds another level of frustration, resentment, dismay, anger or whatever it is he's storing and hides it from you. Then one day, seemingly out of the blue, he explodes. Suddenly he shouts, "You've been doing this for the last two months, and I can't stand it anymore!"

How do you react? How does this outburst make you feel? You're probably in shock. From your perspective, this came from nowhere. You had no idea you were doing anything that was bothering or upsetting your partner. There were no complaints, there was no feedback, there were no hints whatsoever that something was wrong. So what goes through your mind at this point? Probably something like, "Man, I never even knew about this."

The lesson here is this: Don't hold it in. If something is bothering you, bring it up early, as calmly and respectfully as you can. Otherwise, it'll build and build and build, until finally you erupt like a volcano, and your partner has no idea what just happened. This isn't fair to your partner, and it causes fear, resentment, anger and withdrawal. There's no joy in holding things till they get to the point in which you erupt with anger.

Professional Outlets

If you or your partner is doing this, remedial action needs to be taken right away. One or both of you can seek counseling or take an anger management course. Perhaps you've never had the opportunity to learn how to effectively manage anger, a powerful human emotion. Research shows that both prolonged and repressed types of anger are very unhealthy for individuals and relationships. A group class or a series of therapy sessions can help you learn how to recognize anger and deal with it constructively to prevent emotional outbursts or violent behavior.

For me, organizations such as Toastmasters were key in helping me develop speaking skills that has continued to serve me both professionally and personally. I also benefited from Dale Carnegie Training, which offers valuable classes in effective communication and human relations. In addition, you can check the offerings at your local community college, adult education center or research online courses.

With knowledge, training and the desire to do things better, you and your partner will be able to express yourselves effectively and calmly, without reaching a volatile point. Holding things in until you erupt is both bad for your relationship and your health. The solution is effective communication.

Learning to Be a Good Listener

You know what else can make life easier for you and your partner? Learning to be a good listener. Listening is another key to good, effective communication. Real listening makes everything easier in all types of relationships — those with a romantic partner, with a friend, with a business associate, with a relative, with anyone. Unfortunately, here's what happens far too often when we're supposed to be listening: We pick up on certain keywords only, words that we store to use as ammunition later on. This is called selective listening, and in the process of employing this, we completely miss the message.

Say, for example, that we hear our partner call us "selfish." We obsess on this word to the point that we fail to hear the rest of the discussion. Our ears close up, and all we hear is our own mind saying, "Selfish, me? No way, I'm not selfish!" Once the other person is done talking, we turn around and attack, saying something like, "Well, *you* were being selfish when …" Does this accomplish anything? No, it only makes matters worse. The other person might just reply, with complete exasperation, "Were you even listening to what I was saying?"

It's human nature to want to jump in and defend ourselves. But we must be willing to go beyond this natural tendency. We must be willing to hear our partner out completely. There'll be plenty of time to defend yourself later. First, get to the heart of the matter. Give your loved one a chance.

Don't do what Jack does in the next example.

Amanda and Jack, who have been together three months, are having a talk that's going nowhere. She's trying to tell him that she feels uncomfortable around two of his friends. Amanda claims they flirt with her behind his back — behavior she finds immature and repulsive. She feels they are disrespecting her and Jack and the relationship they have. Jack is listening to her words, but he's not hearing the message. Instead of trying to see the situation through her eyes, he starts to get defensive. Let's listen in on their conversation:

Amanda: "Jack, I need to talk to you about something."
Jack: "What's up?"
Amanda: "It's about Josh and Kevin."

Jack: "Hey, cool. I invited them to come over later …"

Amanda: "No, it's *not* cool. I wish you hadn't asked them over."

Jack: "Come on, Amanda. I've a right to invite the guys over, don't I?"

Amanda: "Yes, but that's not what I'm talking about …"

Jack: "You have a problem with Josh and Kevin? You know …"

Amanda: "Yes, I have a problem with them! That's what I'm trying to tell you."

Jack: "I don't get why you have a problem with them. They're my buddies."

Amanda: "I know, but they make me feel very uncomfortable."

Jack: "Baby, you don't need to feel uncomfortable around them. They're my friends. They're just regular, normal guys, you know? There's no need for you to feel intimidated or anything like that."

Amanda: (sighs) "You're not getting what I'm saying, Jack …"

Jack: "I think I'm starting to get what's going on here. You're jealous, aren't you? It's envy, plain and simple."

Amanda: "What are you talking about?"

Jack: "You think I spend more time with them than with you, isn't that right? Which I don't, by the way."

Amanda: "No, that's not it!"

Jack: "Then what's the problem?"

Alberta: "I'm trying to tell you, but you're not listening!"

Jack: "OK, I'm listening now. I'm all ears. So tell me, what's your problem with Josh and Kevin?"

Amanda: "They flirt with me behind your back, and I don't like it one bit. It's immature and disrespectful."

Jack: (laughs exuberantly) "Oh, come on, Amanda, they're just teasing you! You know how they are, always kidding. That's just how they roll."

Amanda: "No, you're wrong! They're not *just* teasing. They're crossing the line. And they scare me."

Jack: "Get a grip, Amanda …"

Amanda: "No, you get a grip, Jack! Don't tell me what to do!"

Their conversation continues, with Amanda growing angrier and more frustrated because she feels Jack doesn't take her concerns seriously. Meanwhile, Jack isn't really listening to Amanda. Thinking she's merely snubbing his friends, he makes light of the situation. He even gets a little miffed, and patronizes her, which then causes her to lose her temper.

Jack is doing a poor job of listening to Amanda and understanding the situation. If he would only listen with his ears, his eyes and all of his senses, he would notice that she's upset with his friends to the point of being wary of their behavior. If he would only listen — really listen — he could take his girlfriend's concerns seriously.

Why did Jack fail to listen? The main reason is he did what most of us do far too often: He became defensive. He interpreted the situation as Amanda attacking his friends. An attack on his best friends was equivalent to an attack on him, and he wasn't about to take that. So he shut down and stopped listening. Meanwhile, Amanda grew increasingly frustrated, angry and disappointed with her boyfriend, who wasn't getting it. Deciding she'd had enough, she left Jack shortly afterward. She simply got fed up with him downplaying his friends' unacceptable behavior. He had no idea why she walked away. If only he had listened.

What's Behind the Pain?

Here's my advice to you about listening to your partner: Do not try to build up your ammunition. If your partner comes to you upset over something, stop, take a deep breath and *listen*. Do so attentively. Give him or her all of your attention. Hear everything he or she has to say. Do not pick words here and there to hurl right back at your partner in defense. Getting defensive will not calm your partner down. It will prevent you from understanding the scope of the situation and the heart of the matter.

Instead of trying to build up your ammo, try to go behind the scenes. What's behind the tears, the frustration, the words and the upset feelings you're getting from your partner? Pretend, for a moment, that you're an objective observer. What do you notice behind the words and the drama? What message is your partner trying to get across? What point is your partner trying to make?

Give your partner the benefit of the doubt. Even if on the surface it sounds as though you're being attacked, try your best not to get defensive. Try to look beyond keywords you find yourself getting stuck on, words like *selfish* or *inconsiderate*. By putting these words aside, at least temporarily, you can find (and focus on) the real meaning behind this conversation. What's bringing on this tirade? What's behind the pain? Why is your partner hurting so much? What's the real message she or he is trying to get through? Listen with patience and with a loving heart, and you'll be more likely to hear what your partner is really saying. When you're willing to listen, you can begin to work toward a win-win for you and your partner.

When to Walk Away

Having said all this, I want to clarify one thing: There's a huge difference between your partner saying something unkind — and later regretted — simply because he or she is upset and hurting, and your partner purposely abusing you verbally or emotionally. Under no circumstances should you take abuse. If your partner exhibits a pattern of abusing you with words, either leave the relationship or insist that your partner join you in couples counseling. Your partner must learn to respect you and stop his or her abusive behavior. If the behavior continues, you have the right to walk away.

If you and your partner are discussing a matter and it escalates into an argument, stop what you're doing. Don't be afraid to take a step back and end the conversation right then and there, before it overheats. Suggest a time out. It's perfectly acceptable for you to say something along the lines of, "Let's plan on revisiting this again later when things have cooled down."

Next, follow through. Make absolutely sure that you do revisit the matter. Put it on the calendar if you need to, but make sure both of you have calmed down before you tackle the topic again. The calmer you are, the better you can listen, and the better chance of both of being heard.

Bring Back the Romance

Nothing kills the romance in a relationship better than a lack of appreciation for one's partner. Even people who mean well and genuinely respect their partner are often guilty of failing to adequately express appreciation.

A woman who was like a mother figure to me once shared with me the following: Her husband was a great guy in many ways, but he failed when it came to communicating. Despite her urgings and nudges, this was one area he didn't care about and didn't have any desire to improve. Needless to say, this was a source of great frustration for my friend.

For example, he couldn't seem to get her birthday right. On one birthday, he woke up in the morning and left the house without saying a word. Moments later, the doorbell rang. When she opened the door, my friend found her husband standing there holding a present. He handed it to her and said, "Happy birthday," then left. So much for that year's celebration. Another year, she woke up to find a blank check on top of the dresser with a note that had the words "Happy Birthday" scribbled across it.

Her birthdays always seemed to be an afterthought for him. In addition to a serious lack of communication here, there was a definite lack of romance. His half-hearted attempts at acknowledging her birthday failed in terms of fully appreciating her and took the romance out of not just gift-giving but the relationship as well.

Romance is purposeful, conscious verbal or nonverbal communication that expresses appreciation of the other person. It doesn't have to cost money. But it does require listening. It's about doing special things for your special someone without being asked. For example, if you hear your loved one complain that her feet hurt from standing all day at work, go ahead and massage her feet. She won't expecting this, and it speaks volumes about you and how much you appreciate her. Your actions say, "I heard you, and this is my response." Now that's romantic!

For many people, listening and taking action to show appreciation doesn't come naturally. That's why you have to practice. It may be difficult, at least in the beginning, but it is doable. Start by practicing intentional listening. Pay attention when your partner is talking. What is he or she saying? What are you learning about this person over time? What are their likes and dislikes? Next, practice intentional, active kindness. What can you do today to make your partner's life a little easier, a little brighter? What can you do to add some joy to his or her day?

Again, I want to emphasize that this doesn't require spending money on your partner. It just requires that you be a good listener and an attentive partner. So go ahead, spoil your loved one a little!

Be Intentionally Kind

Paying attention and taking action becomes natural after a while. Man or woman, you have to look for these opportunities to express your appreciation. You have to listen to things your partner might say in passing and then remember them for future reference. You have to be intentional.

Don't be afraid to be spontaneous and keep the romance alive in your relationship. Make her a cup of tea just because you know she loves tea. Give him a neck rub just because he's had a long, difficult day and this would be such a pleasant treat for him. It's the little things that count.

To me, being spontaneous isn't about guessing. It's about taking calculated action. You're acting off information you already know. With information stored away in your mind, all you need next is a desire to take action. The more you practice spontaneous romantic acts, the more comfortable you'll become with expressing your appreciation in thoughtful ways.

I know some of you will struggle with this. Just like my friend's husband, you might find yourself way out of your comfort zone when you're expected to please your partner through intentional acts of kindness. Don't be too hard on yourself. Perhaps you've never been taught how to do this. Within the Christian society, for example, a man is taught to be a good provider for his wife and his family. But is he taught to listen to her wishes and desires? Often, this essential element is lacking from the religious teachings a man receives, or it isn't emphasized enough. If we haven't been taught to listen to the needs of the person we're providing for, then we need to give ourselves permission to *learn* to listen.

Ease into the Relationship

And now, a word of caution to many of you: If you find yourself being especially romantic and attentive early in the relationship, but after a while the romance starts to die out, try something different. Try easing into romance instead of jumping in. This way, you'll give romance room to grow over time.

Unfortunately, here's what many of us do: In the beginning, we're so excited about this wonderful new person we've met that we call all the time. We call first thing in the morning when we wake up. We call again from work during lunch. Then we call in the afternoon, when we get home from work and one more time at night right before we go to bed.

If you find yourself doing this, be careful — you're setting up a pattern that your partner will come to expect but you can't realistically maintain. After a while the boss is going to tell you to stop making so many calls. Or you're going to fall so behind in other areas of your life that you'll ignore your relationship just to catch up. Meanwhile, the other person starts to worry. Suddenly you're not calling so frequently. Suddenly you're off doing who knows what, leaving him or her in the dark. Your partner starts to wonder what happened. Did he stop liking me? Is she bored of me? Has he lost interest in our relationship? Why won't she call anymore? Where did the romance go?

To avoid disappointing your partner, ease into the relationship. It's better to start slowly and steadily build the romance than to start with a bang, only to watch the relationship suffer later on because you can't possibly maintain the pace you set up. Be careful that what you do in the beginning of a relationship doesn't set a precedent that can't be sustained. Balance needs to be a part of any relationship, and communication is a key part of that. Your guy might want to call you everyday but is afraid of overdoing it. You might want to only chat a couple times a week to make sure the conversations don't get monotonous. Talk to each other about reasonable expectations.

Know When to Compromise

In addition to listening and showing appreciation, knowing how and when to compromise is an important ingredient of good communication. There are countless times in any relationship when you have to be able to compromise. Both partners must learn to do this. Being able to make a compromise in a graceful manner can elevate your relationship to a higher level.

Reaching compromises can take on many different forms, including:

- Volunteering to do something for your partner even if it impacts your schedule
- Forgoing something you really wanted to do because your partner is genuinely tired and needs a break
- Agreeing to meet your partner halfway and asking him or her to do the same for you
- Ensuring your partner's needs are met before yours
- Taking turns
- Giving each other opportunities to make decisions
- Communicating how you feel, asking your partner how he or she feels and reaching a joint decision that benefits both of you, even though each of you has to make some sacrifices

To further illustrate effective compromise, allow me to share a story. Joanna and Bill have been married five years. She's a stay-at-home mom; he works as a delivery person. When Bill comes home, Joanna is dying to tell him about her day, but she refrains. Experience has taught her that he needs a transition period. So after he comes home and greets her and the baby, he either watches TV or reads the newspaper to unwind and make the transition from work to home. After half an hour or so, Bill is ready to communicate. At this point, he willingly listens to Joanna talk about her day. After his break, he's ready to engage in intelligent, meaningful conversation with her. Waiting, then, is Joanna's way of compromising in their relationship.

Meanwhile, Bill understands that he also needs to make compromises to keep things running smoothly in the household. On Saturday afternoons, he takes the baby out to the park, the library or the indoor mall for three hours. This gives Joanna valuable uninterrupted time to herself. This becomes her "recharge" time, when she can watch a movie, read a book, work out at the gym, take a nap or sip a latte at a local coffee shop — whatever she wants to do.

Deep down inside, Bill would rather do something with the baby *and* Joanna, but he gladly makes the compromise so his wife can have a break. Through compromise and understanding, this couple is making the relationship work.

Remember to Practice Respect

Any kind of communication will be effective both in the short term and in the long run if respect is part of the mix.

No matter how upset, mad, hurt or aggravated you are, always do your utmost to respect the person you're addressing. If a person did something that hurt you, allow that person to explain himself. Hear what he has to say.

The notion that you don't have to respect the person, the conversation or even your boundaries because you're angry is completely false. Even when you're distressed, you do not have the right to disrespect another person.

Do you remember the important lesson that Jesus taught us about the most important commandment? Read the following exchange from the Book of Matthew about what matters most:

"Teacher, which is the greatest commandment in the Law?" Jesus replied: "Love the Lord your God with all your heart and with all your soul and with all your mind.' This is the first and greatest commandment. And the second is like it: 'Love your neighbor as yourself.'"

—Matthew 22:36-39, New International Version

Even when you're angry about something your partner did, you must behave in a loving manner toward him or her. You must be respectful and willing to see his or her point of view. But you can't see where your partner is coming from if you're ready to pounce. Instead of attacking, look for the pearl — find one good or reasonable thing in what he or she is saying. When you're able to do this, you'll begin to get to the root of the issue. Give your partner the same respect you would like to receive if you found yourself in the same situation, but with the roles reversed.

Paving the Way for Trust: Tree Trunk Theory

I like to use something I call Tree Trunk Theory as a symbol for communication. Good solid communication requires you stay at the trunk of the tree, instead of veering off and getting lost in one of the many branches. The tree trunk represents being in the here and now. The branches are unnecessary tangents. If you're trying to have a conversation about a particular issue, but your partner digresses into other issues, nothing gets accomplished. It's imperative that both of you stay with the conversation, at the trunk of the tree. Now's not the time to be bringing up stuff that happened weeks, months or even years ago. Don't venture up into the branches; stick with the first issue until it's fully resolved. Then you're free to move on to the next issue.

Listening to your partner, hearing what she or he has to say, expressing yourself clearly and calmly, taking out the guesswork, being willing to learn skills for more effective communication, always respecting each other no matter what, being able to express appreciation and being OK with making compromises now and again — all of these are components of intentional communication. They reveal a certain maturity level, a willingness to reach out to your partner and enter into a deeper, more meaningful relationship. This type of communication paves the way for the next essential element of the FACTS: Trust.

Good communication helps you understand your partner, and it helps your partner know you. When the two of you can look each other in the eyes and communicate from the heart, you have reached a special place in your relationship. You have arrived at the place where trust is born.

CHAPTER 4
Won't Go Far Without Trust

"Trust is the glue of life. It's the most essential
ingredient in effective communication.
It's the foundational principle that holds all relationships."
—Stephen R. Covey

Trust Is Kid's Stuff

Let's travel back to your schooldays — you know, where for most of us, trust was in its nascent stages. There you are, sitting in the classroom, eager and excited at the start of a new school year. New teacher, new classmates, new rules. Everybody in class starts out with great expectations. Even the teacher has high expectations for you. She starts out by giving everyone in the room a one hundred percent. In other words, every student begins with a clean slate. No warnings, demerits or trips to the principal's office. No calls to parents. No missed homework assignments. Not yet, anyways.

A couple of weeks go by, and what happens? Johnny pulls Annie's hair. He drops down to ninety-five percent as the teacher loses some of her trust in him. Erin completely forgets to do a major assignment. She drops down to eighty-five percent. Zach releases the classroom's pet guinea pig out into the playground. He drops way down to seventy percent. Now the teacher finds it hard to fully trust these three kids. But, good and gracious teacher that she is, she gives them second chances. She watches them carefully, but gives them the opportunity to redeem themselves. They can get back up to one hundred percent, but it will take time and effort.

There's not much difference between this childhood scenario and the scenario of dating someone. When two people first start going out, typically they trust each other. Then one or the other person does something to question that initial trust. Building that trust level back requires time, great effort, honesty and no more major mess-ups; at least, not in the immediate future. As we go through life we make mistakes, but too many blunders in a short span of time, particularly at the start of a relationship, can push trust straight out the door.

Trust Is Not Optional

Trust is a precious, fragile thing. It's hard to come by and easily broken. It is perhaps the most challenging of the FACTS attributes. But trust is *not* optional. A good, strong relationship must have it. You simply can't be yourself around someone you don't trust. When you can't be yourself, you end up hiding things from your partner and holding back important parts of your personality. This is simply not sustainable. It's much too stressful to be living a lie.

Much like the schoolteacher in the example at the start of this chapter, when you enter into a relationship, you tend to trust the person automatically (unless you have insecurity or jealousy issues, which we'll cover later). You trust that your partner is telling the truth, representing the person he or she is honestly and accurately, and putting his or her best effort into the relationship. It isn't until this person's behavior or actions fail to match up with what they're saying that you start to lose a measure of trust.

Trust is vital in a relationship because it helps bring out other beneficial factors. When you trust your partner, you can be more open. You can expose your feelings without worrying about having to hide or protect them. You can communicate more openly and freely. By being more open and unrestrained, you can have a closer, more satisfying relationship.

FACTS, Not Fiction: *Trust*
One important aspect of any relationship is to know that you can Trust the other person enough to share what you deeply feel and believe.

It Begins with Honesty

Remember when we discussed how important honesty is to any relationship? Genuine honesty can't exist in the absence of trust. A lack of trust in a partner breeds levels of resentment as well as distance. An absence of trust typically is paired with the presence of jealousy. If Person A is constantly checking up on Person B, questioning whereabouts and accusing that person of not telling the truth, then trust is severely compromised in the relationship.

Perhaps Person B *is* untrustworthy, in which case Person A will find out pretty quickly and muster the strength (hopefully) to end the relationship. But if Person B is genuinely trustworthy, then the fact that Person A *can't* trust him or her speaks volumes about Person A's insecurities. There are countless other scenarios where a relationship ends because trust fails to develop. Let's look at a specific case.

Sharon and Charles met at a church social event. She liked his sense of humor; he liked her warmth and compassion. They began to date and, little by little, they grew to know a great deal about each other. Both were happy to learn that they were compatible in so many areas. Weeks passed and they continued dating, their relationship progressing at a comfortable, pleasant pace to something more serious — until the day Sharon accidentally left her cell phone at Charles' place. A call came in, and he answered it. The male voice at the other end sounded just as perplexed as Charles felt. After this call, Charles immediately broke things off with Sharon. The two never saw each other again.

Up until that phone call, Charles and Sharon were getting along beautifully. Charles appreciated the fact that Sharon treated him with such respect and compassion. They saw each other almost every week, usually a couple of evenings per week, and sometimes on Sundays during one of the church services. He felt a sense of pride being her boyfriend … until that mysterious phone call came in, he learned that Sharon had another steady boyfriend named Dwayne.

Charles learned the hard way that trust was broken. The classy lady he thought he knew so well had deliberately kept him in the dark about the other man. With the T element of the FACTS missing from their relationship, the relationship came to an abrupt end. To add insult to injury, it seemed that just about everyone at Charles' church knew about Sharon dating Dwayne. Everybody knew except for him. He left his church and started attending one across town to avoid further humiliation.

The Mistrust-Insecurity Link

When you don't have trust, you have mistrust, and this is something you don't want in a relationship. Mistrust leads to all kinds of unpleasant things, from closing up emotionally to hardening your heart to worrying about what the other person is doing when you're not around. Mistrust breeds doubt, suspicion, cynicism and — ultimately — distance. A relationship will eventually crumble under the weight of mistrust.

Often, mistrust is misplaced. It can come from jealousy or from a place of insecurity (note that jealousy often stems from insecurity), as in the example of Stephanie and Daryl, who have been dating for three months. They like each other quite a bit and share common interests, including a passion for cooking shows. Daryl is an attractive, fun-loving guy who seems to get along with everybody. Stephanie is a pretty lady with many fine qualities, but she's been in some bad relationships before. These relationships have left her with insecurities and have contributed to her becoming a distrustful person.

When they go out, Daryl usually runs into someone he knows. He greets each person warmly, because it's part of his personality. Stephanie finds herself suspicious and even jealous of each person. She demands to know who each person is and how Daryl knows him or her. At first, he thinks nothing of this. But over time, her suspicions and jealousy start wearing him down. Being around her becomes less and less fun because it feels like she's always accusing him of something.

Over time, Stephanie's insecurities become too much for Daryl to tolerate. He can't talk to anyone without her grilling him for information afterwards. This constant interrogation goes against his laid-back nature. Feeling hurt that Stephanie doesn't trust him despite his high standards and exemplary behavior, Daryl reluctantly calls it quits on this relationship.

Trust Can Be Built

Even if you or your partner is working on insecurity issues, or even if one of you has messed up and lost a measure of trust, the good news is that you *can* build upon trust. Just like the kid who forgot to turn in her homework or the kid who purposely released the guinea pig out into the playground, you can try again. And with sincere, genuine effort to do better comes the opportunity to redeem yourself and regain someone's trust.

Regardless of your past, regardless of how poorly others have treated you before, you can take steps to work on your ability to trust another human being. It might be tough, but you can do it. Believe me when I say it begins with you: You must first work on your own trust issues before you can build a trusting relationship with another person.

If others have said or done things to lower your self-esteem, you must bring that self-esteem back up. Step by step, get to the point of loving and valuing yourself again. Don't buy into the ugly words other people have said. Don't let others' distasteful actions bring you down. You're worthy of living a happy, fulfilling life and being all that you can be. Lift yourself back up. When you can value yourself again, you'll be able to trust others once more.

Ease the Pressure by Creating Balance

After you've learned how to trust again, you can start to bring that trust into your relationships. I know it's hard, but try your best to not be super sensitive. Like a duck, just let some things slide off your back. Let some things go. You don't need to hold onto every cruel or careless thing everyone has said or done. You'll be a happier person when you learn to let it go.

One way to build up trust with your partner is to keep the pressure off. Try going out in different environments; if one doesn't work for the two of you, another will. Instead of seeing your partner alone all the time, the two of you can go out in groups with friends. This often takes some of the pressure off.

At the same time, do make time during the week to spend time talking one on one. A key to building trust is creating balance. When you balance your time with your partner such that sometimes you're alone and other times you're having fun around other people, you'll have the opportunity to grow, learn and trust.

The Three Levels of Trust

You can build upon trust by working on it at three different levels. In Level One, the two of you are simply getting to know each other. Through casual conversations, you talk and learn about each other in a non-threatening way. Trust begins to build over time.

Next, you reach the Level Two, which involves bringing each other into your inner circle. There's more depth to your conversations now, as you begin to share pieces of your life that have greater meaning, including goals and dreams, family stories and even hints of relationships past. Both of you know more about the events going on in each other's lives.

After you've mastered this Level Two, you reach Level Three, which is a much closer and more intimate level. Here's where both of you share more deeply, from the heart, including secrets and vulnerabilities. Yes, both of you are more vulnerable, but more than likely you can handle it. You've built up a great deal of trust since level one, having attained a certain maturity in your relationship where trust starts to become second nature. Over time, you've gotten to know this person, built up trust in your relationship, and allowed this special person into your heart. In an advanced relationship where both people are committed to each other, that's exactly where you want to be.

The Person You Thought You Knew

In the dating world, however, even reaching Level Three in the trust scale doesn't guarantee the success of a relationship. You've let this person all the way in. You trust them one hundred percent and they still end up hurting you horribly. It isn't fair!

Exactly, it's not fair. And it hurts like nobody's business. If you've made it only up to level one with this person, it's not as big a deal. It's like giving money on the street to someone who's down and out. A stranger asks you for money for food. You give in good faith and later discover that he or she has used it for alcohol. You feel used, but you get over it pretty quickly because this person was someone you didn't know. Emotionally, you didn't have much invested.

If your brother approaches you, though, that's a different matter. Say he asks you for money because he's struggling to pay the mortgage. You feel for him — he's your brother — so you give him the funds. Weeks later, you learn he didn't use your money for his mortgage. He spent it on new shirts and tattoos. Now you're hurt, not to mention angry and upset! That's because you trust your brother. The two of you are at trust Level Three. Sure, you can forgive him, but the trust is broken.

This is how it feels when you've let your significant other into your heart, and he or she betrays you. It hurts. Badly.

You thought you knew this person. The two of you were close. You had a deep level of trust. Then he or she goes off and does this to you? Soon you learn that both of you were living a lie.

So where do you go from here?

The Benefits of Seeking a Neutral Party

I must admit, the road becomes unclear when trust has been horribly broken; where you go depends in large part on you. You can forgive your partner, but you may decide you don't want to be with him or her anymore. Or you may want to try to make things work, but you realize that the two of you need professional help.

A neutral party can be very beneficial, regardless of where you are on the trust meter. Whether you're at Level One, Level Two or Level Three — whether you trust the other person one hundred percent or only fifty percent — getting pre-marriage counseling can help you immensely. With a neutral party present, both of you can learn more about each other and tackle issues as they arise. And you can identify whether this is a relationship you want to keep pursuing, or if it's better to end it and move on.

When I say a neutral party, I'm not talking about your mother or your brother or your partner's best friend. I'm not talking about a pastor who's known you since you were three. A neutral party is a counselor or therapist with whom you can be completely honest about everything. If you're in a sexual relationship, for example, you might be reluctant to tell your preacher, "We're sleeping together." But with a neutral party, you won't hold back as much; you'll be much more honest. This honesty is necessary to get to the core of why you're in this relationship and what you want out of it. Honesty is necessary for tackling issues and building trust.

A counselor or therapist is like a doctor — he or she is there to help you. If you can't be completely honest with this person, then I suggest you go to somebody else. Perhaps you can try a counselor or pastor at another church. Or you and your partner can find a therapist in a secular setting. The important thing is that you find someone with whom you can be totally honest.

Only in this manner can you discover your true intent, as well as that of your partner's. Through counseling, you can discover why you want to pursue a serious relationship. You can find out your true feelings about wanting or not wanting to marry the person you're dating. You can better learn each other's likes and dislikes, and you can bring up issues you've been afraid to talk about. You can also pave the way for a much closer, more trusting relationship.

Tactful, Honest and Kind

When I talk about being completely honest, I inevitably get asked whether we should be using a filter. I agree with being tactful; I don't think it's kind or productive to blurt out the first thing that pops into your head. Thinking before you speak is always good advice. But I don't think you should hide your true feelings just to keep from hurting the other person. Sooner or later, your true feelings will come out, potentially bringing a world of pain to your partner anyway.

Like I said, I'm all for being tactful. Don't say, "Your cooking is atrocious!" This may be your honest feeling, but you have to find a better way of letting your partner know that you don't like his or her cooking. Suggest that the two of you take a cooking class, for example. Or offer to prepare a meal yourself. If your partner gets defensive and demands, "What's wrong with my cooking?" don't get sucked into the argument. Instead, find the kindest, most tactful way of letting this person know that there's room for improvement in the cooking department. And it wouldn't hurt to let your partner know that you love him or her anyway, even if he or she isn't a master chef! You've got to be upfront, but do so kindly.

Make Time to Build Trust

Like everything that's worthwhile, building trust takes time. It takes effort. You need to make it a priority. One way to work on trust is by scheduling time to talk. Schedule some downtime to discuss matters with your partner without distractions or interruptions. Create a friendly, open-forum atmosphere that gives both of you the chance to talk. You don't have to do this every day, but once a week or so is about right for most people. This is an opportunity for the two of you to talk about your likes and dislikes, your hopes, expectations and wishes. Remember to be kind and tactful, but don't refrain from being honest.

Making the time to build trust will go a long way in building your relationship. Trusting somebody is about loving them. Don't deceive yourself — if you don't have trust, you can't truly love this person. Hiding your feelings and withholding information, affection and thoughts from someone because you don't trust that person isn't good for your relationship. Scheduling time to talk and share from the heart is a fantastic way to build trust and love.

Trust in the Lord

All right, you might still be feeling insecure, vulnerable, confused. Worse, you might still hurt from trusting someone in the past.

Where do you go from here? Who can you turn to? As always, trust in the Lord. Remember, God is on your side. He wants to see us happy, living a purposeful life where we are using our gifts and serving one another. Of course, God wants what's best for you. So go ahead, place your trust in God.

The Bible offers many passages about the wisdom of trusting God, including these words:

"My salvation and my honor depend on God; he is my mighty rock, my refuge. Trust in him at all times, O people; pour out your hearts to him, for God is our refuge."

—Psalm 62:7-8, New International Version

I've said it before, and I'll say it again: God will not do you wrong. When you're confused by where you stand in a relationship, when you don't know whether to keep moving forward or to call it quits, when you want you and your partner to grow in trust but don't know how to accomplish this, take it to God. Pray for guidance and answers. Trust that they will arrive, when you're ready to hear God's response.

Mistakes and Forgiveness

Maya Angelou, in her incredible wisdom, has said, "The first time someone shows you who they are, believe them." I wholeheartedly agree. But, like Ms. Angelou, I also realize that people do make mistakes. And when you're in a relationship, you can be sure you'll make mistakes, and your partner will make mistakes. My advice is own up to your mistakes. The more honest a person is, the better the chances of working on and repairing the relationship.

Others may give you advice. They may say, "You shouldn't take this." Or they may say, "You should leave this relationship right now." Maybe they're right. Maybe they're wrong. The correct answer is based partly on the situation and partly on what you feel in your heart. You need to pray about it. Ask God for guidance, and listen to God's advice over any well-meaning but perhaps incomplete advice friends may give.

If your partner has done something to break your trust, find a way to forgive. Forgiveness doesn't mean you condone what he or she has done. It doesn't mean you'll forget. What it does mean is you're willing to move forward in your life without holding onto this slight like a ball and chain. You may decide to continue with the relationship, or you may decide to end it. But either way, forgiveness can free you. Getting back at a person out of revenge will not help either of you.

Use Your Judgment

Everybody is different. In every relationship, you need to be a realist, and the reality is that you simply can't have the same expectations for every relationship. Whether you continue to work on trust or you decide to end things depends on many things, including where you are and where your partner is.

It's important to pray about it. See what the Lord says. Sometimes God may say it's better to forget that person. Other times, God might say it's OK to continue with the relationship. You have to use your judgment and try to discern what God is saying to you.

I've come up with my own rule of thumb: If I can't tell that the woman I'm with is telling me the truth, I prefer to move on. If my instincts are right, then the person I'm with will cry, but perhaps in reality, she's merely acting and deserves an Oscar. That sort of person is into drama and manipulation, and I don't think anyone should have to put up with that. Those who purposely lie and deceive as a habit are not worth your time.

When you detect that the person you're with has a character flaw, such as habitual lying or cheating, you have every right to walk away. This person probably won't change, and you need to leave. But if this person messed up and you believe it's a one-time thing, why not forgive and start working on regaining trust? Again, be sure to use your judgment.

Listen to what others say, but in the end, act upon what you feel in your heart, what you believe in your mind and what you feel in your soul. Sadly, I've messed up a number of situations by listening to others. I once dated a woman I liked very much, but I wasn't sure if she was deceiving me. So I talked it over with friends. They were merciless! Whenever I saw them they'd ask me, "You mean you haven't ended it yet? What are you waiting for?" To make a long story short, I broke up with a girl because I listened to my friends. This girl truly wanted to be with me. Later, I learned that these same friends were forgiving their ladies for hurting them. One guy even married a woman who had hurt him pretty badly.

I was younger and more naïve then, but I learned something valuable from that experience. I learned that it's all right to share your concerns with your friends. It's all right to listen to what they have to say. But in the end, you have to use your own judgment. If you listen to others too much, you run the risk of losing sight of what your heart says and losing trust in your relationship. Don't make that mistake.

Monkey Bar Fears

Let's return to the school setting that began this chapter, only this time it's recess and the students race to the monkey bars. Isn't it amazing how easily kids can maneuver on the bars, swinging from one to the next with no fear? Why can't adults be that fearless when making the transition to a new relationship? Instead, so many of us find it hard to let go of what we had with an ex or something we experienced in the past, and we end up not moving forward as a result.

I caution you not to treat relationships like monkey bars, as though you're holding one bar to get to the other. Instead of trying to negotiate two separate rungs — holding one so tightly while reaching for what's ahead — try not to carry one relationship or situation into something new. The goal is to the get to the other side, so you don't get stuck holding both bars.

Too often, we carry situations experienced in past relationships with us into the next relationship. We grip our past hurts so tightly that they become baggage, which only adds weight to our shoulders, making it even harder to maneuver from one stage of our lives to the next, sometimes even paralyzing us. It may be that we stay where we're at because we feel like we have good reason to remain depressed. But I'm telling you now, you have to move forward from things that have hurt you in the past. Whether it's something you observed in your childhood (parents arguing or someone disrespecting a person you care for) or something you did to hurt a former love, not being willing to forgive someone or to let go will adversely affect your next relationship. This approach certainly doesn't aid in being honest and building trust with your partner in a sustainable and healthy way.

When you blame others for far too long, you remain in stasis. The natural inclination is paint yourself the victim and say, "No, you don't understand. When I was a kid, this happened to me …" If you stick with this mindset, you can't move forward.

What you should be doing is blaming yourself for remaining for so long in the same situation. Make yourself accountable: Perhaps say to the person you're blaming, "OK, you did that. I get it. And while I'm sorry it happened, I have to move on." Or, if you don't feel confident to do it face to face, write it in a letter. It doesn't matter if you send the letter, decide to forgive that person anyway, then let it go.

I understand that when things happen that have hurt us, we are wary to risk being hurt again. I've been there. It's like we approach each new situation with a "Nope, I'm not trusting this" attitude. Perhaps you're afraid of being rejected — that the next love interest you meet won't accept something you've done in the past. Or perhaps your current relationship has gone sour and you're afraid of the next one ending badly. Whatever your monkey bar fears, they'll seep into your new relationship, hampering it from the start. Instead, try to assess what you're holding in your heart and see if you can find a positive view on it. For example, from observing other couples arguing (whether they're in your life or they're strangers), you learn what you don't want in a relationship of your own. And if you treat every potential mate as a new person without the same characteristics as people who've hurt you in the past, it's as though you're jumping in with both feet — well, in this case, hands.

Yes, it's difficult to trust when we're making the right choices, because in today's world, we would rather have insurance; we want to know that the person we're with is the right one. But in order to move forward, you have to let go of the bar you're on and trust that you'll land safely on the next one. Besides, God has the ability to move you away from people who will not help you grow, and to move you toward ones who will. so swing away and put your trust in Him.

The Openness Reward

Once you've dared to leave your baggage at the door and enter a new relationship with no fear, you'll be able to build trust with your partner, using the tips outlined in this chapter. Then, when you've reach a higher level of trust with your partner, you can talk about almost anything. You can open up and share from your heart.

It's an incredibly rewarding experience to not be hampered by mistrust and doubt and to just be yourself, knowing that your partner isn't judging you or secretly dissecting the things you say. You reap the rewards of one hundred percent openness.

When you've reached this level, you're ready to master the final attribute of the FACTS: **S**upport.

CHAPTER 5
Lean on Each Other for Support

"Shared joy is a double joy; shared sorrow is half sorrow."
—Swedish Proverb

It Takes Two

In the same way that arches support huge stone walls in castles, cathedrals and bridges, the support that you and your partner give each other can uphold your relationship. Specifically, I'm talking about moral support, the kind that fortifies the spirit and strengthens the mind.

Support is a key component in maintaining successful relationships. It's about encouraging each other's goals and dreams. It's about knowing you've got someone by your side who's willing to help you with what you're trying to do in life.

In many ways, this final element of the FACTS is the cornerstone. Without it, your relationship will collapse. But its presence serves as a unifying force, bringing two people together to a deeper level of understanding and strengthening their evolving relationship.

Engaged in Your Partner's Life

I want to clarify what I mean by support. I'm not talking so much about financial support — although in some cases, and at certain times, this type of support can come into play — nor am I talking about trying to do everything for your partner. I firmly believe that in any successful relationship, each person must carry his or her own weight, to the best of his or her ability. I believe in taking responsibility and serving your role in the absolute best manner possible.

For example, if a married couple with children decides that one parent will work full time and the other parent will stay home with the kids full time, each person is supporting that relationship in unique and important ways. This is something each couple ultimately has to work out on their own.

The support I'm talking about is more basic than this. It's about the two of you knowing that you have a built-in support system with each other. You know your partner's goals, your partner knows your goals, and both of you are willing to offer each other moral support in the pursuit of these goals.

For example, Heather is studying microbiology, while Tim is getting his master's degree in computer science. Now, Heather isn't expected to know the ins and outs of the computer world, and Tim isn't required to know much about biology. But both of them need to show at least some level of interest in the other person's chosen field. Each should be willing to develop at least a cursory understanding of the other's area of study. Not enough to pass a college exam, of course, but certainly enough to be able to follow a conversation. Even more importantly, each person should care enough to know what projects the other is involved in, what big tests are coming up, what milestones have been reached, etc. This way, Heather can help Tim direct his goals, even if she doesn't know much about computers, and Tim can help Heather direct her goals, even if he failed biology in high school.

I'm talking about being engaged in what the other person is doing. It's part of getting to know who this person is, getting to know your partner's likes and dislikes, showing an interest in his or her pursuits and passions. You both need to show a positive, healthy interest in each other's lives. Support can be as simple as that.

FACTS, Not Fiction: *Support*
*You know you're in a relationship with a healthy dose of **Support** when you feel that your partner is allowing you to discuss where you stand, and you give him or her the same right and courtesy.*

Support by Example

Giving support doesn't have to be difficult or complicated. Many times, all the other person needs to hear is "You're doing a good job." Or they simply want to know that you're in their corner; that you're on their side. It's a matter of giving and getting reassurance, encouragement and caring.

Support can be subtle and still meaningful. For example, I have a friend who's a pastor; he has a calm, peaceful demeanor about him. He never has to say anything, but in his own quiet way he's supportive. He sets a good example by how he lives, so much so that one morning, after having met with him the day before, I found myself starting the day by praying. I'd wanted to get into this morning habit for a while. Without saying a word, my pastor friend inspired me to start a new, positive routine.

Showing your support doesn't mean you have to manage the other person's life. Sometimes, simply by the example you set, you're being supportive. The example you set can be enough to show the other person that you're in their corner.

How Lack of Support Snowballs

If you're in a relationship and you fail to be supportive toward your partner, then he or she will feel unloved. The same goes for when your partner shows a lack of support toward you — you may begin to doubt that he or she believes in you. The problem is, when we feel this way, we're more likely to start lying and hiding things. Each lie adds to this snowball you've created, and it gets harder and harder to stop its momentum.

It's a defensive tactic; you're trying to keep your goals, dreams, hopes and ambitions from your unsupportive partner in order to protect yourself. You no longer share ideas and plans with your partner, and ultimately, the insecurity and resentment built up as a result of not getting the needed support could drive you away. Or, it could cause your partner to shut off emotionally from you.

To put this further into perspective, take the example of Josephine and George. By their third date, Josephine thought George was a dream come true — handsome, fun, charming, witty, a good conversationalist and well traveled. Going out with such a classy guy made her feel special.

After almost a dozen dates, Josephine realized that George hardly ever asked questions about her. She knew practically everything there was to know about him, since he'd talked a great deal about his job, exotic places he'd visited, expensive restaurants he'd dined in, movies he'd watched and books he'd read. But whenever she mentioned something interesting she had done, such as having run in a 5K or gone swimming with dolphins, he had little to say and quickly changed the subject.

Josephine continued to try talking about her experiences, which were every bit as interesting as George's. She tried talking about her job, her volunteer work, music she enjoyed, cuisine she liked to prepare. Somehow, he never caught on. He would smile and nod, then shift the conversation back to himself. Whereas once she had found him fascinating and enchanting, she began to find him and his one-sided conversations dreadfully boring.

What's more, whenever Josephine brought up her goals or dreams, George failed to show any support. He either ignored her completely or laughed at her plans. "Why would you want to do that?" he would say, failing to notice how his insensitivity hurt her. He laughed at her college major. He laughed at her first job, which she actually was proud of. He laughed at her dreams and ambitions. Every step of the way, he talked up his accomplishments and belittled hers. Finally, Josephine couldn't stomach his self-centered conversations any longer and ended the relationship.

Listening Is Key

What Josephine had to endure is not an uncommon scenario. It's highly probable that we've all been in a situation in which the person we're dating is someone who doesn't really tune in to what we're about. As we explored in Chapter 3, listening is a key component of communication — and when you've got that down, you can be sure you're showing your partner the support he or she deserves.

It's simple: Try making mental notes so that you can acknowledge and remember the things your partner likes, whether in conversation, in gift-giving, in planning meals or social outings, etc. I'll share an example from my own life experience.

I once told a girl I was dating that my favorite actor is Jamie Foxx. I let her know that I really liked his music too, and at that time, he was coming out with his debut CD and I was super excited about it. When it came time for my birthday, did she buy me the CD? Nope. In fact, she bought it for herself! To top things off, she bought me a dog tag necklace. I'm in the military — Why would I want more dog tags? It's redundant. What's more, there were typos on them.

My disappointment that day wasn't based solely around not getting the CD. It was about my partner not thinking through what I would really like for my birthday. If she had remembered how much I love greeting cards, for example, all she would've had to do was pick out a card and write something meaningful in it, to show me how much she cared. Had I received that, I would've been really touched. That gesture alone would've shown me that she was attuned to my wants.

How Willing Are You?

When you're entering a new relationship, the first question you need to answer is: Are you willing to support your partner in his or her endeavors? It's a valid question, because based on the other person's lifestyle and interests and your own values, belief system and comfort level, you may not want to support them. In some scenarios, you have every right not to, as you'll see in the following example.

Sarah and James have been dating a few months. They get along great and enjoy each other's company. Sarah, however, is starting to feel uncomfortable with James' life goals. He's an up-and-coming rap singer. Problem is, Sarah can't stand rap music. Many of the lyrics and messages make her uncomfortable. Since she likes James so much, she tries to support him, but it just doesn't feel right. Her encouragement feels phony to her. In her eyes, both of them are being shortchanged; he's not getting the genuine support he needs, and she's trying to be someone she isn't.

Sarah asks herself some hard questions: Can I stand by my man and support his musical ambitions? Can I be myself among his rap music friends? Is this the life I want for myself? In the end, her answer to each question is no. Her likes and his likes are not compatible. Knowing that she's not willing to support James and his life goals, she makes the difficult decision to end the relationship.

Make like Sarah and search your conscience to ask yourself, *Am I able to support this individual?* Sure, you may get along well with your partner. Yes, there may be things about this individual you really like. But if there's something that's very important to your partner that you just can't support, then the right thing to do could very well be to call it quits. You might be better off being friends, not life partners.

I can't emphasize enough how important it is to get to know each other early on when you're dating someone. Find out this person's likes and dislikes. Figure out how you feel about this person's interests and life goals. Are you comfortable with him or her? Will you be able to support this person's dreams and ambitions? Can you support what he or she believes in? If your answer to these questions is yes, then you can confidently move forward and actively engage in this particular relationship.

Giving and Receiving Constructive Criticism

How well do you accept constructive criticism? I ask this question because getting support isn't always about the other person telling you everything is rosy. There are times when getting and giving support involves targeted constructive criticism.

I've met some people who think you have to go as far as to lie to be supportive, such as saying, "That's a great outfit," when in reality you think it's hideous. Or saying, "This cake you made is great," when you really don't like it at all. I don't see how that's being supportive. You might be trying to be kind, but in reality, you're being dishonest and misleading.

Being supportive isn't about giving someone false information. It's not about agreeing with everything they say when deep inside you disagree. Come on now, be yourself. Stay honest. Find ways to be supportive without deceit. Don't be afraid to offer constructive criticism when it's warranted.

Say your girlfriend is going on a very important interview, but the outfit she's chosen doesn't suit her. Don't tell her, "You look terrific!" Instead, say something like, "You know you're a winner in my eyes, but I have to be honest, your outfit may not be right for this particular interview." Being supportive here through constructive criticism will help her look her professional best for the interview and may ultimately help her get the job she wants.

Or say your boyfriend is a bad driver. You don't need to tell him he's doing great. You can show your support by asking your brother to give him some driving pointers, for example, or by him yourself about a free driving improvement class offered in your community. If his pride is hurt, you can soften the blow by saying something like, "I care about you too much to let you take unnecessary risks on the road."

As for being on the receiving end of constructive criticism, when your significant other tries to give you advice, take it well. There's no need to get offended or angry. Put your pride aside and listen. This person really cares about you. He or she isn't trying to hurt your feelings, but rather trying to help you. That is the very essence of support. So accept it.

Think about it: Do you really want someone who agrees with you *all* the time? A yes man or yes woman might stroke your ego, but this person isn't going to give you the support you really need to succeed in the long run. So make sure when receiving constructive criticism, you don't become defensive. Defensiveness can make your partner clam up and not reveal feelings, ending the communication flow.

The Two-Way Path to Authentic Caring

The S element of the FACTS is as much about giving as it is about getting. You must have a two-way conversation — not merely a one-way conversation — in order to give and receive support. It's not about one person being selfish and wanting his or her needs met. That just wouldn't work. Support must go both ways. If you're with someone who's only into himself, that relationship will not last long.

I once dated a girl with whom I was good friends and liked a lot. It wasn't until many years later that I realized the unhealthy pattern we were in. Basically, I was her support system but she wasn't mine. She'd tell me she was planning to do something, and I'd respond by telling her whether I felt this was a good decision or a bad one. In other words, I tried to help her out. But whenever I needed her help, I'd receive complete silence. In time, I came to realize that she didn't care about supporting me, that she was a self-centered person. I'm glad I realized soon enough time to call things off.

Take a look at your relationship. Is the other person giving you the support you need? Does the support in this relationship flow two ways or just one way? For support to be flowing between both of you, the two of you must genuinely care for each other. Both need to want to be involved in each other's life. This authentic caring forms emotional intimacy.

A way to be less self-centered and more supportive is to be attuned to your partner's needs. Start paying attention. Tune into your partner's feelings. This requires you to be intentional in the way you pay attention to and interact with your partner.

Call your partner out of the blue just to say hello, even if this action falls outside of your comfort zone. Don't feel the need to relay your troubles or concerns; instead, ask your partner how he or she is doing, and then listen. Really listen. This person is a good friend, somebody you're interested in, someone you've benefited from knowing. Now, try to be there for him or her and ensure the support goes both ways.

For many people, this comes naturally. For others, it takes work. Whatever category you fall into, it's worth being intentional about making a sincere effort to reach out to your partner. Don't make it all about you all the time.

The Good and the Bad: Sticking to It

If your relationship is going well, the two of you like each other, you value one another and appreciate each other's interests, and you seem compatible, then the best thing both of you can do is stick by each other. Have you seen the film "The Pursuit of Happyness?" Will Smith plays a father who's raising his son while battling financial challenges. He and his son find themselves homeless, but through his tenacity and resourcefulness, he becomes a successful stockbroker.

One of the things that struck me about this story is how the main character's wife leaves him and their son in the midst of her husband's personal, professional and financial hardships. That's harsh! It's a scary thing how quickly she leaves him, how easily she called it quits.

Things don't always go well in life. There will be times when things aren't good at all. In some relationships, when everything is going great, you're treated like a hero. It's as if the fans are going crazy on the sidelines cheering you on. But when you fall behind and make a mistake or a poor decision, suddenly you don't hear anymore cheers. Instead, the fans are booing you.

The measure of a good relationship is how well both individuals are able to stick with each other through the bad times — because it's easier to do so during the good. And how well you support one another is a true indicator of how long the relationship will last. A supportive partner who sticks by you helps you to grow and inspires you to be a better person, and that inspiration leads to contentment.

When We Feel Depleted

One thing to keep in mind is that even when you're in a relationship, there may be times you feel alone. The person you're dating just doesn't seem to be there for you. You're doing all the supporting, and you feel depleted. Or perhaps you're between relationships and you feel that there's nobody there for you to lift you up.

I want to remind you that whatever your circumstances, there's always someone there for you, someone who believes in you and supports you through the good and the bad. This someone is God.

When you're feeling depleted, pray. Ask God to restore you. The Bible's well-known Psalm 23 begins with these words:

"The Lord is my shepherd, I shall not be in want. He makes me lie down in green pastures, he leads me beside quiet waters, he restores my soul."

—Psalm 23:1-3, New International Version

In other words, God sticks by you. He leads you to a spiritual place of calm where your mind can be nourished and your soul can be restored. Whenever you feel that nobody supports you, remember that there's always One who does. Pray for restoration, and accept the support that God offers willingly.

And remember to reach out to and talk with positive people. You don't always have to be the hero, the one people come to for help and support. Make sure your circle of friends includes people who give and take. Accept help and support from others.

Journaling As a Support Tool

Can you tell whether you're supportive of the person you're with? One way to tell if you're on track is to keep a journal. It's perfectly fine to be analytical and intentional about offering moral support — in keeping a journal, you can break things down and see how you're doing. Use it as a tool to evaluate your days. At the end of the day, or at the end of the week, check your entries. How did it go? Did you offer support to your significant other? Were you selfless in your actions? Did you think about your partner's feelings? Are there areas for improvement?

Your journal can also help you get to know your partner better. Use it to jot down things he or she says — places she's been to, where he's lived before, foods she likes, music he enjoys, pet peeves, dreams, anything mentioned that gives you a clearer picture of who your partner is. When you're starting out in a relationship, it's especially easy to forget these things. Writing them down will help you remember them, so that the next time this topic comes up, you can recall relevant details. Your date will be impressed that you remember her favorite ice cream flavor or the fact that he spent a year in Nepal with the Peace Corps.

Additionally, you can evaluate how well you support the other person in your prayers, when you meditate, or in your thoughts at night during those quiet moments before you fall asleep. Ask yourself if you're doing all you can to be supportive. Ask God to help you be more attentive to your loved one.

CHAPTER 6
Love Depends on the FACTS

"The most important thing in life is to learn how
to give out love, and to let it come in."
—Morrie Schwartz

Love Is an Action Word

Now that we've studied the FACTS that make a relationship work, we return to what's number one: Love. It's what everyone wants in a long-term, satisfying relationship. The question is, how do you classify love? Is it a feeling? A character trait? A misunderstood romantic sentiment?

Granted, there are certain pleasant feelings associated with love. Passion, tenderness and affection come to play in romantic love. But to succeed at love, loving isn't just about a feeling. Love is an action word. If you love somebody, it takes action on your part to keep that love going strong. Both you and your partner must be willing to roll up your sleeves and do what you need to do in order to keep love alive in your relationship.

That's where the FACTS come in again; they require action. Love doesn't just *happen*. Not lasting love, anyway. You can be instantly attracted to someone, you can feel that you're madly in love with somebody, but in order for love to keep going, day after day, month after month, year after year, you have to take action and keep taking action through the FACTS.

Yes, it takes effort. Plenty of it. But you know what? It's worth it.

The Ins and Outs of Love

It's easy to fall *in* love. We see a pretty woman or a handsome guy who seems to dig us, and boom! We've fallen in love. But it's just as easy to fall *out* of love, because love is fragile. After too many arguments or seeing too many things we don't like about the other person or feeling unappreciated by the other person, we can easily feel that we are no longer in love.

How, then, do we manage to keep love in a relationship when our feelings and perceptions change?

We build love by building on the FACTS. The FACTS strengthen the ties when difficulties arise. Start with a friendship, and keep that going strong. Work on affirming your partner; help him or her guide and affirm you. Communicate regularly, openly and honestly; build that trust between the two of you. And just as importantly, support one another in your endeavors — lift each other up, and just be there for one another.

Take these actions, continue working on these areas both consistently and conscientiously, and guess what? Love will follow. Not the short-term love that evaporates at the first sign of trouble. Not the kind of love that fizzles once you get bored with your partner. But the kind of love that may start out slowly but then grows and grows, and keeps doing so because the two of you keep working on your relationship and put in the time to develop a strong and rooted core.

This is the high-level kind of love the FACTS create. The more you work on developing the FACTS, the easier it is for this love to appear. It's the kind of thing that truly becomes automatic.

Questioning Whether Your Love Is Real

When the FACTS are missing, or they're present but not firmly enough, you'll find yourself asking the question: Is this love? For the answer, consider these thoughts:

- *If I don't think you're truly my friend, how can you really love me?*
- *If you don't affirm me, but others out there do, then how can you love me?*
- *If you're not in my corner supporting me, then why are you here? How can you love me?*
- *If we can't even talk to each other openly and share what's in our hearts, how can we love each other?*
- *If I can't trust you, how can I love you?*
- *If we don't support each other's efforts, does love even stand a chance?*

You'll never know for sure if what you have with your partner is love or simply need, want or desire, right? Wrong! With the FACTS firmly in place, love will become more evident. You'll second-guess less frequently because you'll already know the answer in your heart. Without them, it'll feel like something important is missing, and love will feel like it never quite reaches its full potential.

Succeeding with the FACTS

Eric and Gina had been dating several months when something started to bother him about their relationship. He realized he knew very little about her. She was fun and cute, but he knew nothing about her values, little about her belief system and even less about where he stood with her. They shared common interests, but did they share common principles? And where, exactly, did he stand in her book? Was he just a casual fling or something more?

Sadly, Eric never got his answer. Whenever he started talking about where he stood regarding what he believed in, what was important to him and what Gina meant to him, they'd get interrupted by a call on her cell phone. Instead of turning her phone off or telling the caller she'll return the call later, she took the call, every time. This led to frustration and insecurity on Eric's part. By taking those calls, she was being disrespectful of their time together, and he never got the chance to tell her how he really felt about it. In the end, this relationship went nowhere, and Eric and Gina went their separate ways.

Looking at the FACTS, pretty much everything was missing. The friendship wasn't solid enough for Gina to feel comfortable talking about important topics. She failed to affirm Eric again and again because she chose her cell phone over him. Neither knew how to communicate with the other, with Eric failing to get through and Gina choosing to ignore him. Trust between the two was lacking, since he was too insecure to ask her politely but firmly to put the phone away, and she was too disrespectful and insensitive to allow him to speak his mind. Clearly, support was also missing.

Things worked out better for Sondra and Martin. Mutually, they reached a point where both wanted a deeper, more meaningful relationship. A bit hesitant and just a tad scared, Martin took the lead. He opened up and began to tell Sondra where he stood. He said he really enjoyed her company and felt things were moving along nicely. Martin also said he felt the two of them shared common values and beliefs, and he went on to give several examples. After he was done, he asked, "What about you, Sondra, where do you stand?" Also a little frightened at first, she felt relieved and thankful that he cared enough to share with her where he stood and to ask her the same. They had a three-hour conversation, and by the end of their talk, they felt they'd reached a new level of closeness. The FACTS worked together beautifully in their relationship, and still do to this day.

When Times Get Tough

A relationship is put to the test whenever one person is going through difficult times. Only time will tell whether that person's partner will show sufficient support during these tough times. Take, for example, Jonathan and Lauren. The couple had been together a while, and their relationship seemed to be going smoothly. Lauren worked in a high-stress environment and shared her complaints frequently with Jonathan. "My boss makes my life so difficult," she'd often grumble. "How does he expect me to get any work done when he's constantly calling stupid meetings and giving me extra tasks that have little to do with my job?"

Jonathan would listen patiently and offer words of encouragement and advice, something Lauren appreciated greatly and came to rely on. In Jonathan's eyes, her woes were not that big of a deal, but he wanted to be there for his girl, so he attentively listened whenever she went on about how bad her day was. At the same time, he was relieved that he didn't have much to complain about, as things were going great in his job and his life in general.

All that changed overnight when a co-worker lied to his manager about him. Jonathan was innocent. He didn't do what he'd been accused of, but he nevertheless had to spend the entire day defending himself before a skeptical manager, who finally believed him. Jonathan had never been through anything like that before — first having someone at work lie about him, then having his character questioned and finally having to fight for the truth to be accepted. It had been quite an ordeal.

That evening, when he and Lauren went out to dinner, he shared with her what he had been through. He told her about the embarrassment he'd felt, and the humiliation when his boss believed someone else instead of him. As he spoke, the pain was evident on his face. He'd been through a lot, and at some level he was still processing what had happened, trying to understand the situation and trying to figure out what, if anything, to do next.

When he was done talking, Lauren looked at him with a stone face and asked, "That's it?" Jonathan was taken aback. What did she mean by that? This had been a huge deal for him! He tried once more to explain how terrible he felt, being accused of something he'd never even think of doing. But she brushed him off, saying, "Honey, that's nothing compared to what I went through today …"

As she babbled on for the next fifteen minutes about her workplace woes, he sat in silence. Where was the support? He wondered. After all those times that he had listened to her and offered words of encouragement, why couldn't she return the favor this time? Didn't she feel any compassion or empathy for him? Why wasn't she in his corner supporting him?

Suddenly, he wasn't sure about this relationship anymore. Doubts crept in. From this day forward, Jonathan was no longer willing to open up to Lauren about his feelings, his problems, his innermost thoughts. Her lack of support resulted in him closing up and, in the end, ending the relationship.

Love or Business Arrangement?

When you're in a relationship and you feel there's little support for you, that you're getting more complaints than praise, that you're not being affirmed and that you're just getting put down all the time, you can't help but think, "Man, this person can't possibly love me." You realize that you're part of a business arrangement, not a loving relationship.

In a business deal, both parties agree to certain terms and try to profit from the deal as much as possible. Love doesn't work that way — if you treat your relationship like you're doing business with your partner, you cheat yourself out of an honest, spontaneous friendship built upon trust and open communication.

I've noticed that in recent years, the world of dating has changed drastically. Before investing too much of themselves in a relationship, people want proof that it will work. Unfortunately, this can backfire. We want more proof because we are afraid of getting hurt. We have higher expectations — more often, unrealistic expectations — of our partner. And all of this sabotages the relationship, because we're focused on the wrong elements.

Instead of wanting so much proof, being so afraid of getting hurt and having impossible expectations of the other person, focus your energy elsewhere. Concentrate on building the FACTS in your relationship.

While you're at it, remember to stay open to prayer. Keep praying about your situation. When you pray, ask for discernment, clarity and guidance. Always keep the lines of communication open between you and God.

What the Bible Says About Love

One of the most beautiful passages in the New Testament describes love this way:

"Love is patient, love is kind. It does not envy, it does not boast, it is not proud. It is not rude, it is not self-seeking, it is not easily angered, it keeps no record of wrongs. Love does not delight in evil but rejoices with the truth. It always protects, always trusts, always hopes, always perseveres. Love never fails."

—1 Corinthians 13: 4-8, New International Version

What beautiful words these are. No wonder so many couples include this Bible verse in their wedding ceremonies. Now, take a look at how the passage ties into each of the FACTS:

- Love is patient, the way you need to be patient when developing a **F**riendship with the person you're dating.
- Love is kind, as you need to be when **A**ffirming your partner.
- It does not envy, it does not boast, it is not proud; likewise, you shouldn't be boastful or envious or even too proud to speak up and **C**ommunicate from the heart with your significant other.
- Love always protects and always **T**rusts — just as you need to be able to trust your partner.
- Love isn't self-seeking; instead it **S**upports, a component present in all of the statements in Corinthians above, by focusing on what's best for the two of you so that you can encourage and inspire each other.

I can find no greater summation of what true love is about than in the passage above. Live these FACTS and you'll not only find fulfillment in the foundation you and your partner have built, you'll also be living the Word of God.

In addition to the FACTS, this passage also evokes another quality essential to any successful relationship: honesty. To say that that love "rejoices with the truth" is to represent how important a role honesty play. We'll cover how honesty supports the FACTS in the next chapter.

Seeing Love As the Reward

Love is the reward you get when you take the time and effort to build friendship, trust and support in your relationship, while affirming your partner and communicating openly. In addition, love is what you end up with when:

- You conduct a daily self-assessment to determine what you can do to make your relationship better;
- You're willing to do more than the bare minimum to keep your relationship going strong;
- You try to find ways to better relate to your partner;
- You actively seek solutions to problems; and
- You and your partner are willing to trust each other as you get to know one another and engage in a collective effort to make things work.

One Couple with All the FACTS

There's no doubt that relationships work when all the FACTS are present. I want to share with you the story of two people I know firsthand whose love continues to serve as a powerful model for me. These two people are my aunt and uncle. They've been married for decades, are great friends and still act very much like newlyweds.

For starters, their relationship has such newness and excitement to it. One reason is they never stop working at it. Despite my uncle's demanding career and travel schedule as the president and CEO of a nationwide sales firm, he makes it a point to spend quality time with my aunt on a regular basis. And when he's on the road, their friendship is so strong that they continue to evolve with the times, finding new ways to enhance their relationship by communicating through all forms of available technology.

My uncle even has a rule that his meetings and travel can't interfere with time reserved for my aunt. The way they have it worked out is that from Friday evening through Sunday night, my aunt is his "girlfriend," and Friday night is their date night — dinner, a movie or just relaxing at home. If on Friday afternoon, my uncle finds that a business meeting or deal may run into the weekend, he'll either work into the wee hours that night to finish up, or he'll reschedule completely.

It's always impressed me that their time together carries the highest priority. I remember my uncle saying to me once that sure, he can work on Saturdays, or he could close more deals by traveling on holidays and anniversaries. "But you know what?" he told me, "I'd rather not have the money. I'd rather have quality time with my beautiful wife." It's as though my aunt is his lifeline — as essential to his existence as the air he breathes — and he can't possibly survive without her.

Throughout their vibrant relationship, love stays strong because all the FACTS are being employed:

- They have a terrific **F**riendship, one that has evolved over time.
- They practice **A**ffirmation, and not just during the good times. When they got married, they didn't have much to start off with financially, and their marriage has lasted due in large part to how they reinforce each other's behaviors and faith.
- They **C**ommunicate openly, a true sign of how deeply they respect and care for each other.
- They have a solid foundation of **T**rust: He can trust in the fact that she will be there for him, just as she can trust that he will never let work interfere with their time together.
- They continually **S**upport each other, and are willing to make sacrifices to keep their marriage strong. Luckily, my uncle has experienced phenomenal success in his career, so he's able to continually provide for his family, but he still gets a sense of comfort from my aunt saying, "We can always go back to a small house" or "We can go back to eating hot dogs and baked beans."

My aunt and uncle truly are best friends, and they also have a firm relationship with God, attending church together whenever possible and living God's Word through the way they respect and honor each other.

When you're in a relationship that's so clearly a **F**riendship, and the two of you **A**ffirm each other, **C**ommunicate with each other, and **T**rust and **S**upport each other, that's a relationship worth keeping — and one you want to continually work on.

The Value of Peace

I'm pretty certain my uncle would not be the success he is today were it not for the support and love my aunt provides. Just knowing that she's in his corner makes a world of difference to him. Remember in the film "As Good As It Gets" when Jack Nicholson's character tells Helen Hunt's character that she makes him "want to be a better man"? That's the perfect illustration of the value of peace and how it relates to drive in the mind of a man.

You see, when guys have a stable home and a constant support system, they don't want that to change. When things are good on the home front, positive energy flows from that into other areas of life, so guys are driven to succeed well beyond the standards of what they thought they could do. Just like women, we want someone who loves us based who we are, not on what we can do for that person. By letting my uncle know that material gain isn't as important as being together, my aunt is instilling peace in their home environment. (Conversely, by valuing their time together over material gain at work, my uncle is gifting my aunt with peace of mind.) Having that security in his home life clears my uncle's mind of the usual stresses that hamper many relationships; in turn, giving him the confidence to do his absolute best at his job. That's because when you have love that good, it makes everything else in life so much better.

People thrive on inspiration, and by following the FACTS, you'll inspire your significant other, bringing out the best in that person. You know when you see a couple and you wonder how they ever got together? Perhaps one is far more attractive or much more successful at work. You say to yourself, "How did he get with *her*?" or "How did she get with *him*?" It's because that couple brings out the best in each other, thereby making each other feel invincible.

Truly, love makes superheroes of us all.

CHAPTER 7
Honestly Speaking

"Honesty is the first chapter in the book of wisdom."
—*Thomas Jefferson*

Opening Up As Your Honest Self

In the same way that love emerges naturally when the FACTS are in place, honesty also appears almost effortless when you're friends with your partner, you affirm each other, the two of you communicate well with and trust each other, and you're supportive of one another. Having the FACTS in place allows you to open up to your partner. But just as we've learned with love, honesty can be severely hindered when the FACTS are absent.

Without trust, you can't open up to be your honest self. Without genuine communication and true friendship, you can't trust each other. When you don't receive healthy affirmation or positive support, what happens? You retreat into yourself. You start to hide things and keep stuff from each other, because you're protecting yourself. This may be a normal human reaction, but it doesn't lead to a healthy, honest relationship.

A lack of support leads to a fear-based approach to a relationship. Many people, quite frankly, fear the repercussions of being honest. It's a fear of what can happen, or of how you'll be perceived. It makes me think of a problem a few years back with a motor industry company that needed to fix a particular issue with a car. This company did not want to do a massive recall, for fear of repercussions. Instead, they opted to fix the problem free of charge *only if* people bothered to come in and complain about it. Needless to say, this was a bad situation. What about all those people out there driving around cars that needed to be fixed? Avoiding a recall created a dangerous situation. Similarly, avoiding honesty in your relationship can give rise to problems down the road.

FACTS, Not Fiction: The Honesty Factor

Each of the FACTS is built on honesty. In order to experience true love, you need them all. For example, once you know your partner is supportive of you, you're no longer afraid to tell him or her your dreams. You're able to open up as your honest self.

The Pain of Keeping Quiet

Especially in a new relationship, people are afraid to tell the truth sometimes. They don't want to stir things up by telling the truth, so they keep quiet. But silence can make matters a hundred times worse, in both new and well-established relationships. Nick and Marie had been married for three years. He was the breadwinner while she raised their baby and worked on her college degree. Nick didn't talk much about his job, and he certainly never mentioned any of the crazy happenings going on at work. He always told Marie that everything was fine. In reality, his company was being acquired by another, and his job was at risk. Weeks went by and he said nothing of this to his wife. She assumed everything was great. Without telling him, she enrolled in more classes, but she kept this to herself because she was afraid he'd get angry with her for spending more of his money.

Obviously, this relationship lacked many things: trust, support, communication. The pair didn't act like friends — not real friends anyway. And in so many critical ways, they failed to be honest with each other. They led separate lives, in essence, plowing along, keeping things from each other until the truth could no longer be hidden.

Nick lost his job, just as he feared. He came home that day and said nothing about it to his wife. The next morning, when he didn't get up for work, Marie asked if he was feeling all right. When he told her he'd lost his job, she exploded:

"How am I supposed to pay for my college classes now?" she yelled.

"I thought we already paid for your classes," he replied.

"Not those I'm taking now; the ones I'm enrolled in for next semester," she said.

"You didn't tell me you had enrolled in more classes," he replied.

"Do I have to tell you everything?" she asked defensively. "Do I need your permission for everything I decide to do?"

This went on for a while. When she found out that he'd known for quite some time that his job was in jeopardy, but he failed to share this bit of information with her, she exploded again. Marie spoke harshly to her husband and insulted him in countless ways with cutting words. Furious, he stormed out of the house.

Both had been blindsided by new revelations they'd chosen to keep hidden from each other — he kept secret the fact that his job was at risk, and she kept secret the fact that she had spent money on more classes. Neither was being honest with the other. Neither was being supportive of each other. When Nick returned home, Marie demanded a divorce, which he granted. These two never had a chance. With no trust or support, but with plenty of fear, lies and glaring omissions, their relationship just couldn't survive.

Minimize the Hurt by Telling the Truth

Sometimes, It can be tempting to keep the truth from your partner. It can be tempting to keep things to yourself. But remember, if you don't have the FACTS, you don't have honesty — and you don't have a solid relationship. You have a relationship built on sand instead of rock; it'll crumble when that first storm hits.

Even if you're worried about repercussions, in the vast majority of cases, it's better to open up and tell the truth than to hide things. The only instance I can think of where you really need to protect yourself is if you're in an abusive relationship. In this case, you don't owe the other person the truth — you owe it to yourself to get out safely, the sooner the better. But in all other cases, telling the truth is infinitely better than hiding it. It hurts less in the long run.

Deception Only Leads to Distance

Some people think that the only way to win over a potential mate is to cover up or embellish the truth. *She won't like me if she knew who I really was*, we worry. Or perhaps, *He won't stay with me if he knew what I really thought.* So we begin to create a façade, a fake persona to cover up our perceived imperfections. We fail to tell the other person that our driver's license has been revoked, until they discover it and confront us about it. We neglect to reveal that we're unemployed, until the revelation is made known, perhaps in an embarrassing way.

When we try to win someone over through deception, it always backfires in the end. When the person we're interested in discovers that we've been lying or hiding important facts — and the truth always comes out in the end — we come across as someone who can't be trusted. Lack of trust creates distance, and eventually this hard-won relationship unravels and ends.

There's no need to try to make yourself look better than you are. Don't tell her you're making $100,000 a year when you're earning $30,000. Don't tell him you work as a model when you're really an extra in a film. There's no need to try to be something you're not. If your partner can't accept you for who you are, that's not your problem. You don't really want to be with him or her anyway. Time to move on. Don't compromise your honesty for the sake of starting a relationship, because in the end you'll lose trust and credibility, and lose the relationship anyway.

Being Honest with Yourself

By being honest, rest assured you'll eventually attract the right person to you, the one who accepts you as you are and is willing to listen to your thoughts and feelings. There happens to be a good side effect to being honest; it can lead to positive change. I like being honest because it helps me to make good changes and become a better person. Being honest with yourself requires that you let go of ego attachments to being right all of the time, or giving the impression that you're infallible. Ego or false self interferes with emotional intimacy and authenticity. You've got to be honest with yourself before you can be honest with your significant other. Being honest with yourself first means you're not willing to settle for less.

In the Bible, Jesus is quoted as saying:

"Then you will know the truth, and the truth will set you free."

—John 8:32, New International Version

Indeed, the truth frees us to:
- Be ourselves without fear of repercussion;
- See ourselves and our relationships honestly, without pretext, so that we can change or repair what needs fixing;
- Build trust and strengthen a friendship with our significant other; and
- Live with integrity, knowing we're being true to ourselves and truthful in our relationships.

There's strength and power in speaking and knowing the truth. By staying honest with yourself and with your partner, you succeed in keeping things real and giving yourselves the best chance of success in your relationship. You succeed in taking the higher road.

The right person will love you for this.

CHAPTER 8
Keep God in Your Relationship

"Trust in the Lord with all your heart and lean
not on your own understanding; in all your ways
acknowledge him, and he will direct your path."
—*Proverbs 3:5*

Listening to God's Wisdom

Everything we've covered so far — the FACTS, love, honesty — is necessary for a good, solid relationship. But you'll find yourself at a major disadvantage if you don't keep someone very important in your relationship: God. Stay open to God's presence and guidance, and you'll be in the best position possible to succeed in love.

If the person you're dating isn't right for you, God will let you know. The question is, are you willing to listen? It may hurt to know that this person isn't "the one," but you'll be better off in the long run.

If your special someone *could* be perfect for you, but the two of you first need to make important adjustments for the relationship to work, God will tell you that too. Are you both open to listening to God's wisdom? I hope so, because by keeping God in your relationship, you'll have a huge advantage. This vital connection enables you to consult with the Almighty whenever you get stuck, you need clarity or you wonder if you're headed in the right direction. God wants what's best for you, so why not consult with God? It's in your best interest to do so.

Keep It Real

Is your relationship real, or is it one of those Hollywood relationships, seen so often on television and in movie theaters? In the movies, a guy and a gal meet, they have a fun, whirlwind romantic-comedy kind of courtship and then have their *happily ever after* without having to do any real work. Is this realistic? Of course not. But too many people have these unrealistic expectations in which they meet that special someone and BAM! — everything just magically falls into place.

Folks, that's what happens in Hollywood movie studios, and it's why we love going to the movies: They provide a wonderful, temporary escape into a world of fantasy. In reality, things don't just fall into place automatically. In reality, it takes time, effort and hard work to set a relationship on the right track. It's always sad to me when I see couples going into premarital counseling as an afterthought. The wedding invitations have already gone out, the dress has already been bought, the couple has ordered the rings, as well as booked the florist, photographer and caterer, but they haven't analyzed the relationship to see if they're even compatible. They go into premarital counseling half-heartedly … it's just another box to check before the wedding, just another item to cross off on their lengthy to-do list.

Then, lo and behold, that couple begins to learn stuff about each other. During counseling they begin to see that maybe, just maybe, they're not as compatible as they had assumed. Or they didn't realize what they're getting themselves into — they're simply not prepared for married life. So now what? Do they cancel the wedding? Or, do they go through with it and hope for the best? What a dilemma.

Keeping it real means learning as much about your partner as you can well before you even start to consider wedding plans. Go into premarital counseling early, long before ordering invitations or setting a wedding date. Go into counseling with an open mind and an open heart. As the two of you go through counseling, always keep asking yourselves the following: *Does God have this in His plan for us? Is this relationship right for us? Are we compatible?*

A word of caution: Just because the two of you have God in your lives doesn't mean that you're a perfect match. He loves God and she loves God, but this doesn't mean the relationship will automatically work out. You might your partner's looks, and you might be happy about his or her relationship with God, but what about personality compatibility? What about having other things in common? What about the life goals each person has? Do you share a similar vision for the future? Do the two of you even get along? Just because God is in your relationship doesn't mean it's foolproof … and that's OK. You'll want to know earlier rather than later whether or not you're compatible. So stay real with each other. Get to know each other before you get swept away by wedding preparations. Go into premarital counseling and explore everything about you can each other, from where you're at spiritually to all the practical matters of your relationship. Keep things real, not Hollywood-style.

Why Put God First?

A lot of people, especially young people, wonder, "Why should I put God first in the relationship? Shouldn't my partner be first?" That's a good question, and there are several answers. Putting God first helps you respect each other, and it doesn't mean your partner takes a backseat in your life. On the contrary, by putting God first, you're able to focus on priorities that enable you to put your partner first, too.

Putting God first is a selfless — not selfish — act in which you're dating with purpose, maturity and sensitivity instead of dating just because it seems like a cool thing to do.

When you put God first, you set healthy boundaries, including ones for the physical aspect of your relationship. Often new couples find themselves so attracted to each other that they jump into a sexual relationship without getting to know one other. Then the problems and the confusion start: You meant to put God first, but the physical affection distracted you. As times goes on, you realize that you enjoy the physical side of the relationship, but you don't necessarily like this person. Now what? You're confused as to what to do next. You're torn. You can't undo things and go back to the way things were before you became sexually active. Maybe you're even addicted to the physical side of this relationship, but you're stressing because you know this isn't the person you want to spend your life with. Basically, the relationship isn't going anywhere in the long run.

So how do you call things off? How do you break it gently to your partner that he or she isn't the one for you? Jumping into a sexual relationship before you're committed to each other creates extra complications, pain and emotional injury. By keeping God first, you maintain those healthy boundaries that keep you from jumping into a physical relationship before you're ready. Instead of letting your hormones distract you, you're letting God lead the way. You're getting to know this person in a no-pressure environment — the best way to get to know somebody. You're keeping things in focus instead of being blinded by passion. This approach helps you date with purpose while keeping in mind the long-term potential of your relationship.

In the Book of Matthew, you'll find the following verse:

> *"But seek first his kingdom and his righteousness, and*
> *all these things will be given to you as well."*
>
> —Matthew 6:33, New International Version

In other words, seek God first, and everything else will start to fall into place. Seek God's wisdom, love and guidance. Seek to have a spiritual relationship with God, and you'll see how this in turn helps you in your romantic relationships.

Finding Common Ground in Worship

For me, one of the easiest ways to keep God in a relationship is to make sure I'm dating someone with similar beliefs and standards. We don't have to see eye to eye on everything; it's certainly acceptable to have different interpretations, ideas and philosophies. But when it comes to the basic foundation, it helps to be standing on common ground.

Look at it this way: If one of you is lying flat on the ground, and the other one is standing on a table, it's far too easy for the person on the ground to drag the other person down. It's much, much harder for the person on the table to pull the one on the ground up. Catch my drift? If you're standing on the table, you'll want to date somebody who's also on that table. From there, the two of you can climb up to even greater heights.

Here's my recommendation to you: If you're in a relationship where you see each other regularly, try your best to go to the same church and get involved together in some of the activities offered there. Or at least make the effort to find common ground in worship. If you attend one church, and your partner goes to another one, things can get difficult. I've seen church power struggles between people who choose to attend separate churches. "I'm not growing where he's at; I want to go to a different church," she might say. Or he observe, "We go to your church almost every week, but we hardly ever attend my church." As a result, resentment builds, power struggles intensify and your faith becomes a wedge that's driving you apart instead of a source of strength for your relationship. This is a difficult, sad situation.

If you do go to different churches, then be fair about it. Perhaps alternate, one week at his church, one week at her church. At the very least, find some way to compromise. Perhaps find a Bible study, in which you can participate together. Churches also offer countless volunteering opportunities, so consider getting involved in one or more of them as a couple. Not only will you be doing something good for your community, but you'll also get to see the person you're dating in a safe environment where neither of you is under pressure to get into a physical relationship or to try to impress the other. Instead, you're out there serving the Lord and helping your neighbor — What better way is there to really get to know somebody in a non-threatening, no-pressure sort of way?

The exception to this same-church approach, of course, is when you're in a long-distance relationship. In this case, it's just not possible to attend church together. An online Bible study works really well for long-distance relationships and are fairly common. You can't go to church together, but you can still study and grow spiritually together. This is a wonderful opportunity to get to know each other while you grow in faith, and a fabulous way to keep God in your relationship. By doing Bible studies together, you'll find common ground.

Know Your Happiness

Far too often, we date because we're trying desperately to fill that hole in our heart, to find our own happiness through somebody else. There's nothing wrong with dating someone who makes you feel happy when you're with him or her. But to base your entire happiness on another person is unhealthy and downright foolish. Before you can find happiness with someone else, you must first know your own happiness.

Here's what happiness means to me. I came up with this a while back, and it perfectly sums up the feeling for me:

Happiness is a feeling of self-completion no one can take away from you. It's also a form of joy that includes the Lord's help toward your direction for success.

What's happiness to you? Write it down in the space provided below:

_____

_____

_____

_____

Keep this personal mantra top of mind in all you do, including dating. By memorizing and focusing on what happiness means to you, you'll be able to navigate the dating landscape a little more easily, and a lot less painfully.

Instead of desperately trying to find your happiness in another person, you'll be confident knowing your own happiness already, which in turn places you in a better position to take your time and find someone of substance. In situations where people are happy based off another person but not within themselves, problems arise. One person may resent being held responsible for another's happiness. Or the person ends the relationship, leaving the one emotionally dependent on him or her completely devastated. When it comes to happiness, you need to learn to stand on your own two feet first.

You can learn a lot about people when you ask them for *their* definition of happiness. Try it. Ask the person you're seeing, "What's happiness to you?" Then, take it another step further. Ask him or her, "Name one positive thing and one negative thing about yourself." The answers may be pretty revealing, and will give you important clues about the person's level of self-esteem, self-perception, emotional health and personal needs. The more you know about your partner, the better you can make a decision as to whether there's a shared future for you both.

I can't emphasize enough how important happiness is in a relationship. If you ask the person you're dating to define happiness and he or she gives you a silly answer, you know that much thought hasn't been put into it. But if you get deep answers, or even deep reflection, you know that he or she has at some point pondered the question, "What brings me joy?" or a variation of that. When both of you are ready to address the question, you're ready to explore how you define yourselves, and you're ready to explore a possible future together.

No matter how much you love the person you're dating, or the person you're married to, remember this: No person can fill the gap that only God can fill. It is human nature to jump in and try to fill the holes— perhaps through a loved one, our spouse, our work or a hobby. But it doesn't work that way. People are not perfect; God is. And only God can fill those places in our hearts that need filling. This is the true essence of why we need God in our lives and in our relationships.

The Power of Prayer and Devotionals

Some people might consider this corny, but when you're on the phone talking with your sweetheart, the best thing you can do for each other is to start or end your conversation with a prayer. When you begin with a prayer, it helps you keep your dialogue on the right track. And whether you start or end with a prayer, or you do both, you're keeping your focus on God and you're consciously keeping God in the relationship. This really works well and, in reality, it's not corny at all, because as Christians, we are to pray without ceasing and seek without ceasing. It's not corny when we're following what's written in the Bible:

"Take delight in the Lord, and he will give you the desires of your heart."

—Psalm 37:4, New International Version

Devotionals provide another option. I've seen some people do a devotional rather than a prayer, and vice versa. Others do both. It's up to you.

A good time to do a devotional is first thing in the morning. Other ideal times are right after work or just before going to bed. Actually, any time is good for doing a devotional, so find a time that works for you, based on your personal preferences and your schedule.

For those of you who don't know what a devotional is, the term as I use it here refers to a collection of writings or reflections designed to bring you closer to God. Devotionals are especially effective for people who don't live in the same area or who can't see each other as consistently as they'd like. Being able to share your thoughts regarding a daily or weekly devotional is a great way to stay connected. It will help your relationship immensely.

If you or your partner is overseas or studying at school in another state or away for a long time on business, then a devotional provides you two with something of substance to talk about. You can even spend time on the devotional first by yourself and later, during your phone conversation, share your thoughts and compare notes. This gives the two of you some valuable private time to reflect on God in your life, as well as the opportunity to share your thoughts with each other later on.

Spending time on a devotional topic removes some of the isolation you might feel if you're far away from the one you love. It also is a great reminder that God is with you always, wherever you may be. Even if your schedule is busy, keeping God first by spending a few moments in prayer or devotion — and later sharing your reflections with your significant other — will help you keep your priorities straight. It will bring clarity to your day, and it can even fill you with a sense of calm.

Wherever you may be, it's important that you continue to pray for your relationship or your marriage. Give everything over to God. At the end of the day, simply say, "God, I'm giving it over to you." Take a moment, whenever you need, to talk to God about problems that arise and things that are going wrong — not just the joys of your relationship and everything that's going right.

Fruit of the Spirit

According to the Book of Galatians, we are to live in such a way that we cultivate the fruit of the Spirit:

"But the fruit of the Spirit is love, joy, peace, forbearance, kindness, goodness, faithfulness, gentleness and self-control."

—Galatians 5:22-23, New International Version

The fruit of the Spirit actually collectively serve as an effective roadmap to where you want to be in your relationship. Periodically, check with your partner to see how well the two of you are maintaining these important attributes. Sit down and ask each other, *Hey, how are we doing on maintaining the fruit of the Spirit? How is our love? Are we gentle toward each other? How are we doing on kindness? On self-control? Is there a measure of peace in our relationship?*

This exercise helps you to refocus your priorities and get things on the right track. It brings your focus back to showing love toward each other, on making sacrifices for one other. Let's face it, if you're a guy, sometimes you have to watch one of those "chick flicks" with your lady, even if you don't get the point of the story and you have no idea why the movie is making her cry her eyes out! And if you're a woman who's not into sports, sometimes you have to join your man at the stadium to watch a football game with him. Yes, it's freezing cold, and you're not sure who's playing, who's winning or what just happened, but you're there anyway to support him and his team. We have to make these little sacrifices for each other to keep our connection alive.

One of my friends loves to watch political shows. It's his way of keeping in touch with what's happening in the world. His wife, though, can't stand these shows. She likes to unwind in front of programs like "Jersey Shore." Whenever he watches TV shows that she prefers, he complains that he's losing brain cells! But they each make the sacrifice for the other. She lets him watch his political talk shows, and he lets her watch her reality shows. Instead of making waves, they choose to make small sacrifices to honor each other's desires and habits, because they love each other.

The Greatest Is Love

I included the following Bible passage in the chapter about love, and below I've chosen to reiterate it because it is so important, so beautiful and so fitting for this particular chapter as well:

"Love is patient, love is kind. It does not envy, it does not boast, it is not proud. It is not rude, it is not self-seeking, it is not easily angered, it keeps no record of wrongs. Love does not delight in evil but rejoices with the truth. It always protects, always trusts, always hopes, always perseveres. Love never fails."

—1 Corinthians 13:4-8, New International Version

Plain and simple, true love never fails. God sees to that. Life is about living, learning and loving. Even if your relationship ended, it didn't *fail*. You learned something valuable through your time with this person, and that certainly made it worthwhile. Even if you loved only briefly, you had something precious. Value it, learn from it and apply what you learned to your next relationship.

Keeping God in your relationship helps you stay true to the real meaning of love. If you start to notice things deteriorating, with envy, anger or rudeness surfacing, you can be sure that you need to refocus on God. Try to imagine what God would think of this behavior. How does God want you to treat each other? Why would you allow ugliness to surface in your relationship when, with God's help, you can bring back the love?

Always remember what love really is. Reread the passage above, with particular emphasis on how love "rejoices with the truth" and "always protects, always trusts, always hopes, always perseveres." With God's help, you can make sure that the love in your relationship trusts and protects, sides with the truth and never gives up. By keeping God in your relationship — every day and each step of the way, even when things get challenging — you'll be operating from a place of genuine love. And from this place, the past is forgiven, the present is treasured and the future is filled with hope and promise.

Chapter 9
No Such Thing As Failure

"Failure is only the opportunity to begin again more intelligently."
—Henry Ford

Failure As a Stepping-Stone

Yes, you read the chapter title correctly. *But what about failed relationships?* You ask. What about the times you messed up, made a fool of yourself or inadvertently put your foot in your mouth? Or what about the times you dated someone who was the worst match possible for you, or — perhaps the most awful scenario of all — you broke up with someone only to realize that he or she was "the one." You could just kick yourself for letting that amazing person go!

Aren't these colossal failures? Maybe to society at large they are, but they shouldn't be to you or to anyone else who's serious about dating. There are better ways to look at failures in love. So you messed up; you made a mistake or two. Or maybe you did everything right but things still didn't work out the way you'd hoped. Perhaps the relationship started out great and ended up not so great. But I assure you it's not the end of the world! It's definitely not time to become a hermit and spend the rest of your life in isolation. Instead, use that time to evaluate what took place, what worked, what didn't and what could have gone better, without being judgmental or overly critical.

When you're able to take a good, honest look at what happened, without spiraling into bitterness, rage or any other debilitating, unproductive state, you can learn from your mistakes. There's always something valuable you can take from the experience, and that piece of knowledge becomes a golden nugget of information you can use to improve things in your next relationship — or even in yourself before you begin another relationship. Your "failure" then becomes no more than a stepping-stone along the path to your eventual and inevitable success.

Now do you see why there's no such thing as failure?

Lean on God to Ease the Pain

Before you think I sound too cavalier, I do realize that the end of a relationship can feel like your world has crumbled. The pain from a breakup can be unbearable. You might feel blah and unmotivated, or much, much worse, believing that there's no way you can go on without this person in your life. I understand that kind of hurt and deep pain, but I assure you, you *can* go on, and you *will*.

Don't forget that someone very powerful is on your side. Someone who knows your innermost thoughts, feelings, joys, desires, concerns and troubles. Of course, that someone is God, and He cares deeply about you and indeed has a plan for you. When a breakup hurts so incredibly badly, I want you to remember you're never alone, and you're never abandoned, because God is always with you. Lean on Him in your times of need, and He will carry you forward.

When your relationship doesn't work out and you're hurting, take that hurt to God through prayer. Let God know just how you're feeling. Bring Him your disappointments, your sadness, your broken dreams. God listens. God wants to hear whatever you have to say. Then, after you've gotten everything off your chest, pray to God again, this time asking that He grant you peace. He will.

In your prayers, ask God for peace, for understanding, for wisdom. Before you know it, a sense of peace will wash over you. Answers will begin to appear, gradually revealing why things turned out how they did and, more importantly, what valuable lessons you've learned and how you've grown from the experience. God doesn't leave you stranded. Bring everything to Him in prayer — asking for peace and comfort, understanding, restoration and wholeness — and you'll receive them.

It may take some time, but every day you'll feel a little better and a little stronger, until you're ready to face life with gusto all over again.

This time, you'll be a little wiser, too.

In looking at Scripture, I came across a passage that which instructs us to:

> *"Rejoice always, pray continually, give thanks in all circumstances."*
>
> —1 Thessalonians 5:16-18, New International Version

Now, I've seen many different versions of the phrase "pray continually," — from "pray without ceasing" to "never stop praying" to "keep on with your prayers." But no matter which version you've heard, the message is still the same: Keep talking with God. Keep that connection to the Almighty going strong.

No matter which Bible you study, remember that prayer has to be a continual part of your lifestyle.

Prayer will help take your pain away, and in time, renew you so that you may once again live life to the absolute fullest.

Learning from Failure

Retired four-star Army General and former U.S. Secretary of State Colin Powell wrote, "There are no secrets to success. It is the result of preparation, hard work and learning from failure." Hearing these words from such a wise, distinguished and successful individual makes me feel better. He's right: Learning from failure is key to reaching success in any area of life. Even relationships.

Give yourself some time to grieve your loss and recover. Then, when you're ready, begin the process of evaluating. Take a close look at what you had with your ex. Look at the good parts and the not-so-good parts, and decide where you need to improve for next time.

During this evaluation process, reflect on the following questions:

- *What red flags popped up that you might have missed?*
- *When did things start to change?*
- *What were the sources of friction in your relationship?*
- *How did the two of you handle conflict?*
- *What clues that this person wasn't right for you did you see or hear?*
- *What are some of the things you could have done differently?*
- *How was your connection to God throughout this relationship?*
- *What did you learn from dating this person?*

- *What have you learned about yourself?*
- *With the knowledge you now have, what behaviors will you definitely avoid repeating next time?*

These questions will help you reflect on the relationship. You don't have to answer them in order, and you can focus only on the ones that resonate most with you. Knowledge truly is power. There are hundreds of questions you can ask yourself — not to beat yourself up, but to *learn*. When you know what went wrong and why, you can empower yourself to do things a bit differently next time around. In other words, you can prepare yourself to better handle whatever comes your way.

Even if your next relationship ends with the same or a similar outcome, at least you know what's going on. You know where you stand. You know who you are, what you're looking for, what you'll accept and what you won't settle for. When you've gained this much knowledge, you've succeeded, even if your relationship has "failed."

Knowing what you value and what you want out of a relationship helps you connect with the right person in the long run. Be patient, and don't stress out if things aren't happening for you as quickly as you'd like. Just take it easy, learn as much as you can and remember to have fun along the way. Keep things casual; the less pressure you put on yourself and the person you're dating, the more fun the both of you will have.

If you see a recurring pattern in your relationships that results in losing partners who are important to you, seek a trained relationship therapist or coach to help you break habits that interfere with emotional intimacy.

Return to Prayer

Too many people are so quick to say, *Yes, this is "the one"— this is the person I'm going to spend the rest of my life with!* Maybe yes, maybe no. After only two or three months of knowing each other, there's no way to tell for sure. Intentions may be in the right place, but these people are setting themselves up for disappointment by jumping to conclusions prematurely. Many things can go wrong in this scenario.

For one, prayer often falls by the wayside. I've noticed that when someone too quickly comes to the conclusion that this is *the* person, or that God has arranged this perfect match, prayer stops completely, as if it's not an important part of daily life anymore. It's as though we treat God as a consultant, and when we ignore Him, it's like we're saying, "You know

what, everything's OK in this relationship, God. I can take it from here."
This couldn't be further from the truth.

We all know that the heart can deceive sometimes. In our eagerness
for a lasting relationship, we may grow blind to reason. We may not see
major flaws staring us in the face, so we get off track. The only way to get
back on track is to return to an active prayer life. Don't make the mistake
of dumping God from your life when you think you've found "the one" —
whether you have or not, you're going to need God's guidance and wisdom
to keep you on track.

The Importance of Self-Evaluation

Before you merge your life with another person so that two become
one, you have to know *yourself.* The way to get to know you better is
through self-evaluation. We must look at ourselves and figure out who we
are, what we value and where we can improve.

For example, think about the skills you need to add to your repertoire
to become a better person: Can you improve your listening skills? Do you
need to learn more about current events to improve your conversational
skills? Would you benefit from becoming more patient, more assertive,
more independent, more self-assured, less possessive, less critical, less
negative? Every one of us can improve in some area, and this improvement
can happily benefit our love life, so find time to engage in self-evaluation
and constant prayer.

A good prayer to say when doing your self-evaluation is the
following:

*"Search me, God, and know my heart; test me and know
my anxious thoughts. See if there is any offensive way
in me, and lead me in the way everlasting."*

—Psalm 139:23-24, New International Version

This heartfelt prayer accomplishes several things. It invites God into
your heart and your life, a wise thing to do. The prayer essentially asks
God to pinpoint your worries, fears and concerns. It then asks God to take
the areas that need improvement — anything that is "offensive" — and
lead you toward a better way of living, a way that keeps you on the right
path in God's eyes.

A relationship can end for any number of reasons. It could be something you did. It could be something your partner did. It could be that nobody did anything wrong; the relationship just wasn't right for you. It may be you both agree you'd be better off as friends than as partners.

Nevertheless, as part of our self-evaluation, we need to ask God to search in our hearts. We need to put pride aside and ask these questions humbly: *Did I make any mistakes? If so, what were they? Did I do anything that may have been an offense to God?* This probing is necessary because you want to make sure that anything you may have done that's regarded as offensive is removed from you. God will gladly help you through this process of purification, to prepare you for your next relationship.

Allow the Seasons to Pass

I can't stress enough how ridiculously easy it can be to dive into a relationship too quickly and enter a fantasy state. You know the one, where we think the person's perfect, the relationship is solid, nothing can go wrong, and then — surprise, surprise — things don't work out. The problem? We're living a fantasy, not real life.

The solution? We need to wait before committing. Not twenty years (you probably have commitment issues if you're waiting that long) but long enough to allow the seasons to pass. I know people who say, "It's been six months. Why aren't we married yet?" And to that I ask, "What's the big rush?"

My advice is to take your time. Ecclesiastes 3:1 tells us "there is a time for everything, and a season for every activity under heaven." Try to see that it's OK to get to know the person; it's OK to let things unfold naturally. There's no reason to rush. There's no need to set artificial dates or start worrying when six, seven or eight months have passed and you're still learning about each other. The worst thing you can do is rush the relationship. Take it slow; savor the seasons that pass as you get to know your partner better. In time, you'll have your answer. Either this is the person you'll spend the rest of your life with, or this is a delightful individual who was meant to be in your life for just a few seasons. Perhaps the purpose of the relationship is to learn something to take away and apply in your next relationship. After enough time passes, you'll know. Rushing things won't get you any closer to where you need to be. It'll only put unnecessary pressure on the relationship and cause anxiety.

If you find that the two of you have no future together and need to go in different directions, remember that you're not a failure. Either way, you tried — and you should commend yourself for it. You've learned lessons and gained valuable life experience. So regardless of the outcome, you've emerged a winner.

Discover Each Other's Wants

Another good reason to let enough time pass before reaching a decision is that both of you need ample opportunity to discover each other's wants. You're not considered a failure when you aim to truly understand what the other person wants in a relationship. If you find out you want kids and she doesn't, or vice versa, you're not a failure — it's actually a good thing you discovered this early in the relationship before you've made a lifetime commitment. If you find out he insists you join his political party and you don't want to, or vice-versa, then once again, it's better that you know upfront.

It's vitally important that the two of you make it clear what your understandings, wants, and true expectations of the relationship are. Sometimes in the excitement of dating and just being with another person, you overlook covering the important stuff. Eight months in, you're picking out your wedding dress or practicing how to pop the question, but you don't even know where the two of you stand on questions that will have a major impact on your lives once you're married.

These are just some of the topics you'll need to discuss before you even dream about wedding plans:

- **Starting a Family**: Do both of you want to have children? If one of you does and the other doesn't, then marriage may be out of the question. If you decide you do want kids, then ask more questions. How many? Biological, adopted or both? How long do you want to wait before having children? If you want to wait no more than a year before starting a family, but your partner wants to wait at least five years, can you work this out? Can you reach a compromise both of you can live with?

- **Working**: Where will each of you work? Do you share compatible ideas with regard to jobs? If one of you is heavily career-oriented and the other isn't, how will this impact your relationship? If you have kids, will one of you stay home with them? Will both of you share in the childcare responsibilities?

Do you plan to adjust your work schedules so that you can take turns staying home with the kids? Is this plan feasible? How will you make it work?

- **Finding Common Ground**: If you're a Democrat and your partner is a Republican, does it matter to either of you? Do you expect each other to share political views, or can you coexist peacefully even with widely differing views? If one partner plans to attend political rallies and picket lines, would the other be supportive? Do you see eye to eye on religious matters? With regard to belief systems in general, what do you have in common? Can you accept having a spouse whose viewpoint may be the opposite of yours? What if she smokes and you don't? What if he's a vegetarian and you're not? Can you live with these differences? Can you still find enough common ground upon which to build a solid relationship?

Before you launch into a major commitment, make sure both of you understand each other's expectations. In the sample questions above, for instance, if your partner is highly involved in political causes, think long and hard about whether you'd be fine with receiving a phone call at work from a friend saying, "Hey, turn on the news! Your wife's in a tree that's about to get bulldozed!"

I've mentioned in earlier chapters how important it is to have the opportunity to observe the person you're dating around his or her peers and family. Nowadays, so many of us are in long-distance relationships. We meet online and see each other infrequently. Or we go away to college, get stationed by the military or travel for work, forcing us to do the long-distance thing. In these situations, you may think you know each other when you really don't. Until you see your partner interacting with friends and family in his or her own comfortable environment, you may not know him or her very well. Observing your partner around people he or she knows and trusts gives you a broader view. You get to understand your partner better. You get to see the bigger picture.

Don't Let Your Past Get in Your Way

For the longest time, I had a pet peeve: I wanted people to say things to me a certain way. More specifically, in a kind, nonjudgmental way. If I felt even a hint of accusation when they addressed me, I tried to correct them. *I didn't do anything wrong, so I shouldn't be accused, right?* I went out of my way to talk to others in a diplomatic, attentive and respectful manner, so why shouldn't I get the same courtesy in return?

It wasn't until recently that I learned there was much more to my pet peeve than I realized — it was a product of my past. You see, when I was 14, my mom left my dad. After that, my dad took care of things for us kids, but it wasn't the same. My mom's absence was definitely felt. Even when she came back six months later to settle the divorce, by that time, my abandonment issues left me feeling out of control of the situation. In my 14-year-old eyes, nothing was guaranteed.

This lack of control and trust affected me profoundly, even later as an adult in my dating life. In my efforts to establish myself as a leader, I struggled whenever my partner took issue with something I said. This aggression was residual from my mom's behavior before she left, and if I felt that the person I was dating lacked compassion or understanding, I'd get nervous that she would leave me someday as well. I had a hard time trusting my partner. All because I'd been hurt before.

At work, I took issue with anyone who questioned my decisions. Also, if I said I'd do something, I did it. In fact, I took great pride in being on point. I made it clear that I was in charge, and anyone who questioned that would have to answer to me.

As you can guess, this approach did not win me any friends or improve any of my relationships! That's because whenever I felt like someone was questioning my ability to be a capable leader — whether they really were questioning me or I was simply imagining it — I became defensive. *How dare they question this about me? Don't they know what I've been through?* This last question is irrational, because no one knows what we've been through, yet we still ask, *Don't they know me?*

Once I finally realized what was really going on — that my insecurities from my mother leaving my father affected my ability to tell the difference between a simple question and a perceived attack on my character — it was life-altering.

A self-evaluation showed me that it's my issue. Most importantly, it showed me that I had the power to correct it. So today, with my changed outlook and adjusted expectations, I've been able to steadily improve myself, which will only serve me well in my future relationships.

What about you? Are there unresolved issues or insecurities from your past surfacing in your life? How are they affecting your interactions with others?

Our past experiences can affect how we interpret what our partners say or do. For example, a simple statement or question can be blown way out of proportion. To see why you're overreacting, look to your past for clues. Once you discover which insecurities are being triggered, you can take steps to change how you react as well as your perception. You can finally stop letting your past sabotage your present.

Healing from past wounds is an essential element to experiencing emotional intimacy in our relationships. When we have unfinished business, it blocks our ability to experience mature love.

Gain Perspective Through a Spiritual Parent

So what *is* a big deal in a relationship, and what isn't? If he leaves dirty dishes in the sink without washing them, is that a big deal? If she leaves clothes all over the floor without picking up after herself, is that a big deal? How do we know when we're making a big deal out of nothing?

It's easy for us to lose perspective. At times like these, a mentor comes in handy. I call this person a Spiritual Parent, and in my opinion, everyone should have one. A Spiritual Parent is somebody who's been married a long time — someone who's been there, done that. It could be your aunt or uncle. It could be your godparent. It could be a trusted family friend. Your Spiritual Parent can help you see if you're on the right track in your relationship. And because this is a person you know and trust and who has been married a long time, he or she is the best candidate for shedding light on your situation.

Before you say or do something you'll regret, something that may possibly ruin your relationship, check with your Spiritual Parent. Go ahead and vent: *She leaves her makeup, lotions and perfumes all over the counter and I can't stand it! He can't make a decision without analyzing everything. Why can't she be more spontaneous? He only knows how to cook three dishes; why won't he learn how to cook something new?*

When you talk with your Spiritual Parent about what's bothering you about your relationship, you'll learn that these types of issues are normal. As you talk with your mentor, you'll see what he or she has been through in his or her marriage, and you'll see that most stuff isn't really a big deal in the grand scheme of things. Your mentor might tell you it's OK if your boyfriend isn't a sharp dresser, since you can work with him on matters of style a little at a time. Your mentor might tell you not to worry if your girlfriend doesn't share your taste in music — that over time, your own musical preferences will evolve anyway.

In other words, your Spiritual Parent helps put things into perspective for you. Your mentor can share stories about his or her own pet peeves and learn-to-live-with compromises, as well as any struggles he or she experienced early in marriage and how they were resolved. Your mentor's insights can salvage a relationship that's going through some speed bumps. He or she can help you see what is and isn't a deal breaker. When it's really not a big deal, your Spiritual Parent can tell you, "It's OK, that's just a minor thing. You can work through it."

When seeking a Spiritual Parent, find someone who'll be honest with you. Make sure this is someone you respect and trust. Your Spiritual Parent will offer valuable guidance and suggestions, and you can always take it or leave it. But if I were you, I'd listen carefully to the useful information he or she is trying to impart. After all, your Spiritual Parent's marriage has passed the test of time, so you know the advice is reliable.

Remember, you don't have to learn everything the hard way. And you certainly don't have to go it alone. A Spiritual Parent can offer you shortcuts to important insights that will help you in your current relationship as well as future ones. Remember to thank your mentor for his or her willingness to help you.

CHAPTER 10
Give It Your Best Shot!

"You have to accept whatever comes, and the only important thing is that you meet it with the best you have to give."
—Eleanor Roosevelt

Your Personal Best

There's a quote I like to refer to that's widely used in our world today. It often surfaces in business, in motivational seminars, in movies and in countless other circles:

"If you're going to be a bear, be a grizzly."

—Mahatma Gandhi

Were you just as surprised as I was when you saw that this quote is attributed to Gandhi? Wouldn't you agree it's the kind of quote you'd expect from a high-ranking military officer or an imposing business mogul, not a pacifist?

The more I thought about it, the more this quote made sense to me, and the more I could see that someone like Gandhi — known throughout the world as a deeply spiritual man who modeled empowerment through nonviolence — would have said it. After all, the quote isn't about dominance and aggression. It's about being your personal best.

The grizzly is considered by many to be the most ferocious of bears, therefore representing the highest level of the bear family. So to me, the message behind the quote is: *Whatever you do, do it to the best of your ability.*

In every relationship you enter, always give it your best shot. Do your best to develop and apply the FACTS: **F**riendship, **A**ffirmation, **C**ommunication, **T**rust and **S**upport. Be strong like the grizzly and work on establishing that satisfying, rewarding relationship you've always wanted!

Don't Settle for Less

The above quote intrigued me enough to do a little research on grizzly bears. Here's one interesting fact I discovered: A grizzly will go after larger mammals than themselves when they're available. In other words, grizzlies aren't afraid of animals that are bigger than they are. Two parts of this fact stood out for me: "go after" and "when they're available." How do I translate this into life in general, and relationships in particular? How about the following:

When you're giving it your best shot, don't settle for the small things in life. Go after what you want, and truly believe that you should have it when God makes it available to you.

Just because you encounter an opportunity or a situation that's bigger than you are, don't be afraid to go after it. Pay close attention to the last part of my interpretation of Gandhi's quote, the portion that I consider to be vitally important: Make sure God endorses what you want. If He doesn't, then have the wisdom and grace to stop going after that goal and move on. If God does make your wish available to you, then go after what you want! No need to hold back out of fear or insecurity.

Why settle for less when God is making more available to you? I ask this question especially to those of you who feel stuck in a dead-end relationship. If you're unhappy dating this person, why are you settling? Why don't you believe in yourself? Don't you trust God to help you find someone who's right for you? I suspect this last question in particular will strike a chord with many of you, especially when you begin to fear that you won't find someone new. But God has a plan for us all.

To me, settling is a matter of *willingly* deciding to give up on your dreams, feelings, goals, standards, principles and future in exchange for a false hope of receiving someone who, or something that, was never intended for you.

Let's decipher this further: When you have a willingness toward something not intended for you, it makes you more prone to rely on a source outside of The Source, who is God, our Living Water. Relying on any source outside of God means you've allowed yourself to settle, so you've essentially cheated yourself out of a full life and a full connection to God.

Think about that. Let it sink in. Once you've fully grasped how relying on an outside source equates to settling, you can no longer claim to be a victim! All you have to do is plug back into God — your life energy source — and you can get your power back.

Letting your dreams and your future rely on false hope is a dangerous precedent. You find yourself believing in something so much, it becomes unhealthy. You fail to see that you're on the wrong path. Blind trust in false hope prevents you from seeing a situation clearly; it can drive you in the opposite direction of common sense. This is what can happen when you settle.

Instead of settling for less, actively work on developing more of the FACTS within yourself and in your relationship. If God approves of your current relationship, the FACTS will strengthen your connection to this person, drawing the two of you closer. If God doesn't want you with this person, the FACTS will help make this obvious. By maintaining an active prayer life, you'll be more attuned to what God has in store for you.

Stand Your Ground

Another known fact about grizzlies is that when they're too large to climb trees in the face of a threat, they'll stand their ground. They're so sure of themselves that they'll face their challenges rather than run away. How can this be applied to relationships? Simply: Don't run away from challenges. Face them directly, with confidence in who you are and what you've learned. Stand your ground, knowing that the Lord is by your side.

Having the FACTS in place — **Friendship, Affirmation, Communication, Trust** and **Support** — helps you stand your ground instead of running away at the first sign of trouble. Stay strong in your relationship, just like a grizzly. Give the situation the time it needs before figuring out whether to proceed or call it quits. Sharing where you stand with one another is an act of courage and love that involves genuine honesty and all the elements of the FACTS. If all of the FACTS plus love and honesty are alive and well in your relationship, then it'll be easier for both of you to share where you stand with each other, every step of the way.

Put yourself in position to be your very best. Carry yourself with respect and dignity. Hold on to your values. If your relationship comes to an end, don't fret. Despite your good intentions and high hopes, this person was not a good match for you. Don't treat it as a failure; regard it as a valuable learning lesson. If the relationship continues, you can be sure you've reached a deeper level of closeness and understanding.

Even in the best relationships, challenges appear. Instead of giving up and running away, stand your ground and face these challenges knowing that you've got God backing you up.

Avoid Being Overly Guarded

Try not to be overly guarded after a breakup. I understand the tendency to do so is common, however I have a friend who is recently divorced. Certainly, this person is experiencing a lot of pain and a great deal of mistrust — and understandably so. He came up with a plan that I find unrealistic and potentially harmful. He decided to make it a rule that he must fall in love three times before considering marriage again. To me, this is a poorly conceived plan, an attempt to run away from emotional intimacy while playing the dating game.

The truth is, we don't need to run away. God didn't give us a spirit of fear. We can walk in authority as we seek solutions. That way, whether a relationship keeps going or ends, we'll know that we've given it our best shot.

Power Through Rough Patches

Dating can be fun, but it also can be trying, and even discouraging, at times. Don't let the rough patches get you down. Anything worthwhile takes some work to attain, even a good relationship, so try your best to power through.

When you're feeling discouraged, think about the following Bible verse:

> *"We are hard-pressed on every side, but not crushed; perplexed, but not in despair; persecuted, but not abandoned; struck down, but not destroyed. We always carry around in our body the death of Jesus, so that the life of Jesus may also be revealed in our body."*

—2 Corinthians 4:8-10, New International Version

Yes, Christ is with you — within you — as expressed poignantly in the above Bible passage. You may be going through some very difficult times, maybe even a painful breakup or one broken relationship after another. Ultimately, something will work out for you. In the meantime, you can get active and start building up the FACTS in yourself so that you can then start bringing them into your next relationship.

Avoid the NASCAR Urge

Have you ever watched NASCAR? Those drivers travel at amazing speeds. So fast, in fact, that the drivers' reaction times aren't always quick enough to avoid accidents. If you ever feel that way in your relationships, you're not alone. I call it the NASCAR Urge: We're often moving so quickly that we don't have time to react. We don't have time to pray or listen to God's counsel. Sometimes all we hear are the voices that distract, the voices of doubters and naysayers.

Slow down! No need to race like those NASCAR drivers. In the end, they're just going around in circles anyway. You may be going at warp speed in your relationship, but are you really going anywhere? Or are you just going around in circles? You may think you're going fast and making progress, but it's likely you're not.

Stop going in circles and start taking your time. Actually, try getting out of the driver's seat. Instead, get in the backseat and let God be the driver. Now that you don't have to worry about that NASCAR Urge anymore, you can concentrate on prayer, on your own personal conversation with God. The slower you go, the less you'll rely on people who don't necessarily give the best advice for your situation — and the more you can rely on God.

Messages for Success

Looking back at the beginning of this chapter, how can we reinterpret Gandhi's bear quote to make it relevant to our lives? Below you'll find a list of axioms I compiled that can be applied to any aspect of life, including dating and relationships:

- *If you're going to dream, dream big.*
- *If you want to achieve a goal, go after it with all you've got.*
- *If you want to succeed in life, be the best you can.*
- *If you want a healthy, happy relationship, get the FACTS!*

You're on Your Way!

Now that you're up on all the FACTS, you're more than ready to try the tips and pointers presented in this book and apply them to your own life. You can develop the elements of the FACTS — **F**riendship, **A**ffirmation, **C**ommunication, **T**rust and **S**upport — in yourself and in your relationships. As you do, you'll watch love and honesty grow on the foundation of the FACTS. You have an exciting journey ahead of you!

I would like to share with you a few parting thoughts. First of all, remember that you *can* succeed in love. Get the FACTS, get real, stay strong, give it your best shot and go the distance. Success truly is within your grasp.

Next, always keep these key tips in mind:

- Give your relationship time to develop.
- Don't jump into love — get to know the other person.
- Maintain your true values — don't compromise on these.
- Move slowly; the slower you move, the more time you'll have to solidify your relationship.
- Don't pay attention to fleeting, dubious so-called "signs."
- Rely on a solid foundation of the FACTS and your constant communication with God.

And lastly, remember to stay strong. Like the grizzly.

The Importance of
Ministering and Serving

"When you're part of a team, you stand up for your teammates.
Your loyalty is to them. You protect them through good
and bad, because they'd do the same for you."
—*Yogi Berra*

Marriage As a Ministry

At the core of the definition of ministry, you'll find the word service. Therefore, when you enter a new relationship, try bringing to it a mindset to serve. In fact, think of your relationship as your own personal ministry.

Marriage is indeed a ministry, in which two people come together to serve each other and look to God as their ultimate support system. When you begin to view marriage as a ministry, it changes your whole perspective. You stop being so concerned about yourself and your own needs and realize you're part of a greater calling to serve and support someone else. You stop trying so hard and instead just do your best.

In fact, if you tell yourself, *I'm going to do the best I can to serve the needs of my partner and give this relationship 100 percent,* you'll be setting the tone for success. But while you should always attempt to give 100 percent, you'll find that some days are harder than others. Perhaps on a particular day, the best you can give is 10 percent. That's OK, because as long as you're giving the best you've got, your partner may be able to give the remaining 90 percent to pick up your slack. You just need to let him or her know by communicating how you feel.

However, this doesn't mean you should get too comfortable, to the point of relying on your partner to handle certain aspects of your relationship all the time. For example, just because your partner is better at planning trips doesn't mean that you should expect him or her to do so from now on. And whenever we overextend ourselves, it doesn't give us a free pass to skip out on little things like grocery shopping or writing thank-you notes. Avoid one-sided behavior by always offering to help out.

In practice, ministering is about looking for the need on both sides, so both you and your partner should get in the habit of seeking opportunities to help each other when either of you has an off day. Try to share accountability in your ministry to ensure that your relationship is still growing.

Elijah and the Widow

There's a story in the Bible about the prophet Elijah asking a widow for water and a piece of bread. In reply, the woman made it clear that she barely had enough flour and oil for herself and her son, who were on the brink of death. Elijah assured her to not be afraid; he requested that she make some bread for him and for herself and her son. The Lord spoke through Elijah, assuring her that neither her oil nor her flour would run out.

The woman did as Elijah asked and was able to feed him, her son and herself for days. Then, when her son became ill and stopped breathing, Elijah returned the favor: He helped the widow and the boy by restoring the boy's life through prayer. The kindness the widow had selflessly extended to Elijah came back to bless her and her son in an amazing way.

To me, this biblical account illustrates clearly that in all things, and at all times, we are called to minister and serve. Helping others is part of our daily walk. And part of being of service is being supportive toward others. It's about putting other people's needs before your own. It's about genuinely caring about the person you're seeing and watching out for his or her wellbeing.

The widow in the story was down to her last bit of flour and oil; nevertheless, she was willing to say, "I'm going to help this person, even if I may not get anything out of it." Much the same way, we are called to support one another, even if there may not be anything in it for us. To reach the next level and truly support a loved one, we must to be willing to give and help, even if we don't know if we'll get anything in return. How well we're able to do this is a measure of true love.

Life As a Golf Ball

Throughout life, we all seem to go through a period in which we are searching for our greater purpose — God's plan for what we are meant to do. In the meantime, we're so hard on ourselves about our imperfections, including the things we don't do well. I recently saw a TV program about the history of golf, and learned that were it not for all those dents, golf balls wouldn't be capable of traveling the distances they do in a typical match. And here I had thought the dents were just an aesthetic design; I had no idea that golf balls were specifically *built* to go far.

This got me thinking: Until you know your purpose in life, it's easy to look at your imperfections as hugely noticeable, just like dents on a golf ball, and be ashamed of them; or worse, let them stand in your way of finding happiness. But I assure you, once you find your purpose, you'll realize that, like a golf ball, you were built the way you are by God to be able to smoothly travel through the figurative hills and valleys of life that are laid out before you.

Note that I said hills and valleys. I could've said "greens," but life isn't as neatly laid out as a golf course. We all experience its ups and its downs. But you know what? We were built to handle them both. Having read this section, I bet you'll never be able to look at a golf ball the same way again! I actually hope you don't — I want that golf ball to remind you to stay on course. I want it to make you realize that you're fully equipped to handle whatever comes your way, including trials and tribulations. I want it to reassure you that those tough times do indeed serve a purpose.

Share Your Story

As you go through your journey with the FACTS, please feel free to share your story with me. It's part of my own ministry to have shared this book with you — spreading God's Word as well as what I've learned from my own experiences in love — and to continue the conversation further to help you draw conclusions, get answers to your questions and put the ideas in this book into practice.

I encourage you to not only explore my website (where you can read and comment on my blog, review my published articles, check out my bio and get the latest news and event info about this book), but also join the conversation with other fans on my author page on Facebook and my Twitter feed:

www.getthefactsbook.com
facebook.com/JermaineHamwright
twitter.com/jaysonhamw

Twitter hashtag (to use when chatting about the book):
#FACTSbook

On each of these sites, I frequently post thought-provoking observations, relationship tips, inspirational quotes, Bible passages and news about the book. I would love for you to visit and share what's on your mind or simply say hello!

With Gratitude

From the bottom of my heart, I thank you for reading my book. I hope you've learned some things to help you in all your relationships as well as in your search for a long-term partner in life.

You've likely learned a lot about yourself along the way, and I encourage you to never stop learning. It's of the utmost importance that you know who you are and trust that God will indeed guide your path.